Blowers,
Bubbles
& Balls

To Tony Best wishes MDoT Henry Blofeld

Blowers, Bubbles & Balls

Henry Blofeld

Illustrated by Bill Mitchell

WP
WYMER
PUBLISHING
Bedford, England

First published in Australia in 1984
This edition published 2016 by Wymer Publishing
Bedford, England
www.wymerpublishing.co.uk
Tel: 01234 326691
Wymer Publishing is a trading name of Wymer (UK) Ltd

ISBN 978-1-908724-43-4

Henry Blofeld portrait © Steve Ullathorne.
Courtesy of Emma Brünjes Productions.

Printed and bound by
Clays, Suffolk, England

A catalogue record for this book is available from the British Library.

Cover design by Andy Francis.

Contents

ACCIDENT OF BIRTH

When looking back on life, a great many of us settle on one incident, one piece of luck, good or bad, which started the ball rolling in an upward or downward direction.

My own mind settles unerringly on 7 June 1957 when, with great skill, I elected to ride a

bicycle into a bus, which was going at a fair speed, and succeeded in being knocked unconscious for more than thirty days.

By the time you get to the end of this book you will have discovered that this has been by no means the only time in my life that I have been the victim of unusual circumstances, most of which have been entirely my fault.

Going back to the summer of 1957, I was captain of the Eton College cricket eleven and a batsman wicket-keeper of some promise. The year before when I was still sixteen, I had slogged a hundred for the Public Schools eleven against the Combined Services in their annual two-day game at Lord's.

Nowadays, that may not sound much of an achievement. But I shall immediately say in my defence that there were a number of first class cricketers in the Combined Services side and when I came in the score was 72 /6. And, while I am at it, the only two other schoolboys ever to have done it before were Peter May and Colin Cowdrey, both of whom went on to captain England.

The bus I ran into was bringing a party of robust members of the French Women's Institute to look round Eton, so at least I ensured that their outing had a memorable start. I was bicycling to nets immediately after what was known as Boys' Dinner but which was seldom a culinary gem. Head down, I was crossing the narrow Datchet Lane which runs between two of Eton's most famous playing fields, Upper Club and Agar's Plough.

The bus was approaching from an easterly direction. I am told by my great friend Edward Scott, now chairman of John Swire's in Australia, who was just behind me and who showed outstanding competence as a Casualty Officer, that it was quite a party.

It was well into July and after a number of brain operations - they say they did not take too much away - before I took any further rational interest in life. By then too, any chance of the sort of future in cricket which that hundred at Lord's may have suggested had been bashed with me into the wooden palings at the side of the Datchet Lane.

After profiting considerably from the joint brilliance of a brain surgeon and a plastic surgeon, I was considered fit enough to go up to King's College, Cambridge, the following October. You see, I had had one great piece of luck. The accident had made it impossible for me to take an entrance exam which I would almost certainly have failed and King's took me on trust - a decision I rapidly made them regret.

I have always tried to persuade people that it was simply because I was no good at exams, but for some extraordinary reason there were those who were prepared to doubt my enthusiasm for Medieval Economic History and similar subjects. I have always felt this was a wholly unchristian attitude on their part. The long and the short of it was that I failed my exams in both my first two years at Cambridge. In point of fact I was awarded a technical pass in my second year, but that was not good enough for a college with such high academic standards as King's.

But, by a great fluke, I managed to acquire arguably the worst cricket Blue to have been awarded since the war when I scraped into the 1959 Cambridge side as an opening batsman of a sort. Still, I suppose in view of what happened later it was an important gain from two otherwise ill-spent years. They ground finally to a halt in the course of a charming interview with the senior tutor of King's. He shook his head in a sorrowful way which suggested all too strongly and 'I'm sorry, but there is nothing else that I or anyone else can do,' attitude and proposed that it would be best for me to go on to 'the next thing in life'. In other words...

As far as I was concerned the next thing in life might have been selling ice creams. I had not the faintest idea what I wanted to do, but, lo and behold, a marvellous rich uncle stepped in, just the way marvellous rich uncles are always meant to.

While my family breathed deafening sighs of relief, I was enrolled as a trainee in a merchant bank in the City of London. I acquired three suits with waistcoats, a gold watch chain (but no watch to put on the end of it, of course), a number of stiff collars and, believe it or not, a bowler hat which I still have somewhere as a memento of one of the least favourite parts of my chequered career. I probably had a rolled umbrella too.

I may or may not have looked the part, but I soon discovered that it was most emphatically not a role I wanted to play. I started off in amongst the huge ledgers in the general office under the watchful eye of Mr Sutherland, moustachioed, rising towards middle age, and a veritable pillar of rectitude. I can't think what he can have made of me. For two and a half years I moved around the building, upstairs and downstairs. My only solid achievement was to find, until my bank manager forbad it, a passionate interest in the progress of incurably slow and obstinate horses.

Merchant banking and I were clearly not cut out for

each other; that was easy to see. To find a rational alternative was an altogether different problem and one to which I now put my mind, or what was left of it.

The first alternative which occurred to me was the wine trade, probably because of a great fondness for the product which I had developed early in life. Mercifully, for my liver at any rate, those whom I approached were very much less keen on me than I was on them.

At the end of much soul-searching I came to the conclusion that the only thing I had ever been any good at was cricket. It suddenly occurred to me one evening, almost certainly after I had had too much to drink, that I might be able to write about the game. For some reason, it did not worry me that I had never written a single sentence for publication except for an account of a second eleven soccer match between Eton and Bradfield. This had landed me a pretty swift and sharp interview with Robert Birley who was headmaster of Eton when it appeared in the Eton College *Chronicle*.

We had played a game against Bradfield on their ground near Reading. First, they entertained us to a lunch of 1957 public school culinary expertise and then beat us on a pitch which we had discovered at the top of a steep hill and which looked like those photographs of the Battle of the Somme without the casualties. It was muddy. I shall never forget the sentence which caused the trouble. 'After eating what passed for a lunch, Team B climbed a steep hill and found what was left of a soccer pitch.' So, in a sense, I had scored a libel action first time off. My vice-captain, left back and probable literary collaborator, was the aforementioned Edward Scott.

Anyway, having come to the conclusion that my future lay in finding and following a 'literary' career, I wrote with all speed to some cricket writers I had met and back came the inevitable answer - 'Go and work for a provincial newspaper as a general reporter and get some experience.'

Then, one day at the end of May 1962, I returned home after dinner to find a telegram had been pushed through the letterbox. It said simply that I was to ring a number in Longparish, Hampshire, and was signed Woodcock'. Johnny Woodcock was the cricket correspondent of the London *Times* and he was one of those to whom I had written.

I called him at once and heard that one of his paper's cricket writers was ill and his Sports Editor wanted someone to write about a county cricket match between Kent and Somerset the following two days at Gravesend.

I said 'Yes' as fast as I possibly could. He told me to go straight round to Printing House Square to meet John Hennessy, the Sports Editor, and to get my specific instructions as well as a press ticket. I did so with breathless excitement. When I got home soon after midnight it suddenly hit me. I had undertaken to write four hundred words each day about a first class cricket match without having so much as a semicolon's worth of experience behind me. I tossed and turned a bit that night.

In the morning I called my office in the City and told them I was ill. Then, I drove to the Bat and Ball ground at Gravesend with all the authority my first press ticket had given me. My self-confidence had diminished considerably by about five o'clock when I had to start writing my first-ever piece. By the time I picked up a telephone to dictate my four hundred words through to 'Copy', it was fast approaching nervous breakdown time.

As the evening wore on I could only see my newfound career tumbling down around me as I became increasingly convinced that a worse cricket report had never been written in the entire history of the game. It was another sleepless night with my poor wife who had been forced to share the smallest double bed in the world which had found its way into a seedy hotel in Rochester.

By half past six the following morning I could stand it no longer. After dressing stealthily, I crept out into the metropolis of Rochester to try and find a copy of *The Times*, perhaps not the most frequently read newspaper in those parts. The first two bleary-eyed newsagents I came across were not pleased to see me and told me that they had none over from those which had been ordered. I struck lucky at the third and feverishly paid over the sixpence or whatever it was in those days. Clutching the paper tightly in my hands, I now made a big effort to keep calm. But my heart was beating as if there was no tomorrow as I lengthened my stride back to that miniscule double bed.

This was probably the worst moment of all. There I was with the moment of truth no further away than the length of time it would take me to open the sporting pages of the paper in my hand. Should I look now or when I got back? Was I a genius or had it all been a pipe dream?

After about twenty yards I could stand it no longer and frantically tore open the paper. And there it was, an ordinary, normal, anonymous (no by-lines in *The Times* in those days) cricket report of four hundred words.

I recognised the first paragraph as my own, saw one or two other familiar phrases and tore back to the hotel feeling as though I had achieved the literary equivalent of climbing Mount Everest. When I got back to bed, I collected myself and read every word of it with much greater pleasure than I ever get today from reading something I have written. It was all there.

I doubt if Shakespeare himself felt quite so pleased when he saw *A Midsummer Night's Dream* in print for the first time as I did that morning in Rochester.

All went well the next day too and the following Sunday afternoon those in charge of these things at *The Times* called me and asked if I would do two more days for them the next week. Flushed with success I accepted instantly and rang my office the next morning and said I was ill.

Those two days also passed without any major disasters and the following Sunday I had the temerity to ring *The Times*. I was told that there was five days' work for me in the coming week. I made a note of it all and in the morning I called my office in the City and told them I had left. I spoke to the General Manager whose name was Joe Paine and who was altogether too school-masterly and 'goody-me' for my liking.

He asked me what I meant.

'Simply that I am not coming in again,' I replied. And I did not.

So that was how it all began.

THE HENRY BLOFLY
STAND

An enormous amount of water had passed under the bridge by the time I walked into the Sydney Cricket Ground early in January 1979. I was on my fourteenth major cricket tour as a writer and a broadcaster, I had just had a row with the *Guardian*, my main newspaper in England, which had only narrowly avoided being terminal, but I was enjoying my way of life more than I had ever dreamt I would on that first distant day at Gravesend.

This now was the scene of the Fourth Test match between England and Australia in the 1978/79 series. If I was feeling a little bit pleased with myself as I walked into the ground, it was, I suppose, because having arrived in Australia with almost no work to do, I had had the luck to pick up plenty since.

One of my new jobs was to be interviewed, face to

camera, on ABC Television. On the first day of the First Test match in Brisbane Peter Meares had asked me if he could interview me during the tea interval. He wanted someone who would put across the English point of view.

Our first chat seemed to go pretty well and we had one or two good laughs. The upshot was that I was asked to do an interview again the following day. Again, it went well and after that it became a daily event through the series. We always managed to have a good laugh and a legpull in amongst all the serious stuff.

Usually, I had a go at him and he took it all in a marvellous spirit, although once or twice I had him nicely red in the face. But, in fact, he went on to win the legpull stakes by a distance one teatime during the Adelaide Test in late January.

I climbed rather shakily, for I was still nastily hungover, up the scaffolding to the television platform at the Cathedral End of the loveliest ground in Australia for our daily encounter. I had had a particularly heavy night and I felt lousy. Knowing that I had a reputation for playing hard in the evenings, which is of course monstrously unfair, Peter was less than sympathetic.

Looking me straight in the face without the tiniest flicker of a smile, he started off, live too, 'Henry, you're not looking at your best today. The trouble with you is that you spend too much time in bed and not enough time asleep.'

For the first and, touch wood, the only time in my life I was left completely speechless and, worse than that, I felt myself blushing. After several false and stuttering starts, I think I said very hesitantly something like, 'Yes, Peter, I don't think I know what to say about that.'

By the time I walked into the Sydney Cricket Ground early in January, I had appeared no less than thirteen times in these face-to-camera interviews. Sometimes they had stretched for seven or eight minutes but more often they lasted only for three or four. It was another job, and, as long as my bosses were happy, so was I. I enjoyed these chats immensely, but it was hardly the stuff that heroes are made of.

Back at the SCG, I climbed up the interminable concrete steps in the Noble Stand to the press box. The game had been going on for more than an hour when either Tom Prior of the Melbourne *Sun* or Rod Nicholson of the Melbourne *Herald*, who were sitting together, said to me, 'Blowers, have you seen what's on the pylon on the Hill?' There was a white sheet round the bottom of it covered in red lettering. I borrowed some binoculars.

On all the Test grounds in Australia spectators stick up banners proclaiming the fame of their heroes. The corrugated roofed shelter at the back of the Hill was called the Peter Toohey Stand and then in small letters underneath, 'Such a brilliant batsman, they've named a brewery after him.' Toohey was a successful New South Wales batsman and Toohey's is the name of a big brewery in Sydney. A few years before, this shelter was invariably the Doug Walters Stand and once it was probably the Don Bradman Stand.

Six floodlight pylons had been put around the SCG so that cricket could be played at night and one of these was in the middle of the Hill. I got the sheet in focus and the huge red capital letters said simply, 'The Bespectacled Henry Blofly Stand'.

It was a moment or two before it sank in that this referred to me. At first I felt rather embarrassed, but then I began to realise that it was the most tremendous honour - although cricketers are always honoured in this way, no one could remember a journalist getting his name on the Hill before. It was the result of my daily teatime stint on television during the Test matches and amazingly, five years later, notices to Henry Blofly are still stuck up on the pylon during Sydney Test matches.

Besides the television, I was also writing a daily column in the *Australian*, Rupert Murdoch's national daily. After I had rung my copy through that night I learned from the Sports Editor, Mike Jenkinson, that he had decided to use a photograph of the Blofly Stand on the back page.

The next morning I was early to the ground, having bought just about every copy of the *Australian* I could lay my hands on. I was immediately set upon by hordes of small boys who wanted my autograph. It was heady stuff and was all right by me.

'The Bespectacled Henry Blofly Stand' notice was in place that morning too, and there was a second sheet which said in equally large letters, 'Henry, come on over and have a pint. ' In the circumstances, it was nothing less than a royal command, and I decided I would go round after lunch.

By that time word had filtered back to the Sports desk of the *Australian* and a photographer had turned up to make the journey with me. As I left the press box I found Jack Fingleton sitting just outside. He at once began to pull my leg and then said he would bet that I wouldn't dare go round.

Jack had a marvellous pithy sense of humour and I shall never forget his first ever remark to me in Australia. I was sitting in the press box in Perth in October 1968 when Jack came in. After I had said hello to him, he looked at me with a broad grin and said, 'Blofeld, take those marbles out of your mouth.'

I assured him now that I was already on my way round to the Hill. He looked at me and smiling again said, 'Blofeld, I'll bet you won't dare go round to the Hill wearing that Iz tie.' I was wearing the Izingari tie, which is one of the most conspicuous of club ties with its wide orange, gold and black stripes. I think I would have taken it off, but after Fingo's remark I had to accept the challenge. So, I merely loosened it and undid the top button of my shirt. As I was about to walk on, Fingo spoke again, 'I don't know what they'll make of an Old Etonian over there.'

I must admit I wasn't altogether sure myself and I was a little bit nervous about it all, but after the Hill had paid me such a compliment and had issued a public invitation, there was no way I could refuse it.

First, the photographer and I had to collect passes which would allow us to go from the Members' area into the Outer. With these in our hands we climbed up the slopes to the Paddington turnstiles. After closely scrutinising our credentials, a highly suspicious gateman allowed us through into the Outer. We emerged through the gap between the Bradman stand and the old Bob Stand, so named because it once cost a shilling to sit there.

The path went in front of the Bob Stand and behind all those spectators crammed in behind the boundary pickets. We were in the open and almost immediately it began. First, a lone voice shouted out, 'There's Henry Blofly,' and then it was taken up everywhere.

The cricket was pretty dull with England struggling to stay in the game in their second innings after Geoff Boycott had been out to the first ball and the crowd were happy to find a diversion. The game was being watched in near silence. As I walked on towards the Hill, the crowd all round me began to shout and cheer. At firsfl felt very embarrassed. No one was more surprised than the players themselves and they all turned round to see what on earth was going on.

People now began to run up and shake my hand, and I was asked to sign a great many autographs. By the time I had reached the end of the Bob Stand and had started to walk along the path at the bottom of the Hill towards the floodlight pylon, I was causing quite a disturbance. By now I had got over the initial shock and the feeling of embarrassment and was enjoying every moment of it, for it was all so marvellously good-natured and friendly.

'Come and have a beer, Henry Blofly,' was coming at me from all sides. A number of spectators came running towards me with cans of beer in their outstretched hands for there was no restriction on bringing in booze in those days. By now, the chaps who had stuck up the Blofly Stand sign were busily waving at me and cheering me on.

Then, I began to climb up the thickly populated grassy slopes of the Hill and everyone seemed to be shouting at me and laughing as I picked my way through. It was the most incredible experience and one I shall never forget. An important Test match was going on and yet there was I the centre of attention on the Hill.

Soon, I was pumping the hand of Chris Saxon and the founder members of the Bespectacled Henry Blofly Stand. There were never less than ten people talking to me at any one time, or so it seemed. Questions were fired at me almost as fast as I was offered cans of beer and there was some good humoured rivalry from the members of the neighbouring Peter Toohey Stand.

The guys who had put up the Blofly Stand sign all seemed to be at university. They told me that the idea of the stand had come to them after watching those interviews on the box. Apparently they had reckoned that I had always been fair to both sides and they liked the way Peter Meares and I had a laugh. They told me too that they thought I had kept the bullshit to a minimum.

The only doubt they seemed to have about me was

the length of time it took me to polish off a can of cold beer. I was just starting on my second when an attractive girl with dark hair came running up, threw her arms around me and kissed me and, not content with that, she told me that she would like to marry me.

I told her I thought it was a great idea, but she then damped my spirits a little by saying that, while she would settle for me if she had to, Geoff Boycott was the husband she was really after. Then, she added insult to injury by asking me if I would give him the message. At that time my relations with Boycott were strained, to say the least, which was not an unusual position for a journalist to find himself in. So I suggested that I might not be the most persuasive of messengers. But she was quite undeterred; she showed me exactly where she was sitting and said she would expect him after the tea interval and went and sat down.

There was one mildly hostile incident. About ten paces in front of us a man, who was soon to show that he was drunk out of his mind, rose very unsteadily to his feet with a full and unopened can in his right hand. He lurched towards us and from about a few paces away yelled a forceful and probably highly threatening sentence at me, all of which was incomprehensible gibberish. Then, with some deliberation while he took aim, he hurled the can at me. It just touched my shoulder. His mates took only a matter of seconds to sort him out.

We now got on to some pretty heavy cricket questions as to whether or not Kerry Packer was good for the game. Then another girl, younger than the first and in fact too young, came up and made another proposal of marriage. I told her that I thought we ought to think about it a little longer and discuss it again perhaps on the next England tour to Australia. She seemed happy enough to leave it at that and accepted a cigarette as an immediate substitute.

While all this had been going on the photographer had been clicking away relentlessly. After a few more posed shots it was time to leave for I had to be back for my next telephone broadcast. After another round of vigorous handshakes and a quick chat with Chris Saxon, we were off, threading our way back down the Hill.

The cheering and the shouting began again. I was offered a can of beer every yard I went and received hundreds of invitations to pay a return visit. I only wish I had been able to spend the rest of the day on the Hill, for they were all so wonderfully friendly. But that broadcast beckoned and I had to move on.

The next day there was another sign up which said, 'Our Henry can even outdrink Keith Miller.' Keith still hasn't sued for libel or defamation as far as I know. While I was on the Hill, Chris Saxon promised he would give me the original Blofly sign when the match was over. He and his friends ran across the ground at the end of the match, holding the sheet between them. When I went down to see them, one of them said to me with a laugh, 'I'll tell you what mate, we're not half getting short of fuckin' sheets.' I have the sheet at home in Norfolk and it will always be one of my most treasured possessions.

By the following year, when England were again in Australia, the Henry Blofly Club had been founded and the membership card had on it a copy of the drawing of me, made from a negative, which the

Australian used with my column. I had my dark glasses on and it made me look as if all I needed was a white stick or a guide dog.

I was presented with card number 007 which I would have thought was hardly appropriate for a man with the name of James Bond's arch enemy. The year after that I had a party for the Henry Blofly Club at the Sebel Town House and each year more signs have been going up on that floodlight pylon.

We have had, 'Henry Blofly doesn't even pay for the sheets,' and then there was, 'Henry Blofly is to cricket as Tony Greig is to limbo dancing.' And on the Saturday of the Sydney Test in 1982/3 we had, 'Henry Blofly asks if Irving Rosenwater has scored with Wendy Wimbush.' Irving scores for the Channel Nine commentators while Wendy keeps the figures for the ABC commentary team. Actually, I plead not guilty to the charge of asking an unanswered question.

All I can say about the Henry Blofly Club is, long may it continue and to those who had the original idea, thank you for the honour, and for all the fun it's been.

THE NAKED TRUTH

Travelling round the world watching cricket at the same time as living life as fast and furiously as I can, has made for a highly adventurous, diverting, exhilarating and, at times, dangerous existence. Along the way I have got myself into one or two scrapes I could happily have done without.

A few years ago, I had spent ten days travelling round England watching county cricket while writing and broadcasting and moving on from one modern high-rise hotel to the next. I was going by train at the time for my car was on one of its periodic visits to hospital.

Eventually, I arrived in Nottingham where I was going to stay for two nights and booked myself into the large and fairly nasty hotel overlooking Trent Bridge Cricket Ground but they were only able to have me for one night. I asked them if they would find me a room somewhere else for the second night. Accordingly, they booked me into the Albany Hotel in the middle of Nottingham and I clocked in there at about eight o'clock in the evening. I was shown up to my room on the ninth floor where I had an outstanding view of smoking chimneys and low clouds and nothing that was too strongly reminiscent of Robin Hood.

I had a bath, put on a clean shirt and went down to an excellent dinner and an even better bottle of wine. I did not go to bed until I had finished my book sometime after midnight and the trouble began almost immediately I reached my room. I undressed quickly and went straight to bed. Ever since those in charge of my fortunes when I was a child had allowed me to forget about my pyjamas, I have slept stark naked.

I suppose I had had a certain amount to drink for I went to sleep like a good 'un. But I woke suddenly at three o'clock, realising that I had to respond pretty sharply to an acute call of nature. As these things render further sleep impossible until they have been dealt with, I leapt out of bed without turning on the light and befuddled with sleep made my way to the bathroom.

Now, in these hotels all the rooms are more or less alike and the bathroom is nearly always in the same place '. At least it had been for me on the previous five nights and I went unerringly to the door where once again I expected to find everything I wanted. I opened it and went straight through and looking out through the slits in my eyes, I could see that it was an odd shape.

There was a wall immediately in front of me and the room seemed to stretch away for ever to the left and the right and I couldn't see any of the usual offices. Then, suddenly, I heard the ominous slam of the door behind me. It jerked me sharply to my senses.

You've guessed it. I found myself standing stark naked in the middle of the ninth floor corridor with my watch showing me that it was just before five past three in the morning. I was in a bit of trouble. Being thick with sleep as well as bursting to take off ballast, I was not perhaps at my best for taking instant and far-reaching decisions. Rather hesitantly I set off to try and find a fire escape or maybe some stairs, but it was no good.

The situation was looking increasingly bleak, to say

the least, when I suddenly spotted a tea tray in an angle of the wall just outside another bedroom door. I examined it and under the cup and saucer I found a paper napkin folded into quarters. Feverishly, I unfolded it and held it in front of the offending part of my anatomy. It was just about all right and nothing stuck out round the edges. The only avenue of escape now left to me was the lift. I pressed the button, intending to go down to the ground floor and give the night porter the thrill of his life.

The lift responded splendidly to my summons and I jumped inside. I saw from the buttons that there were fourteen bedroom floors numbered from fourteen down to one. Below the figure one was a button marked R which stood for restaurant, below that a B for bar and finally another R for reception.

With great care, circumspection and precision, I pushed the bottom R and the door shut. I took up my position in the back of the lift, facing the doors with both hands in front of me holding the napkin in place. We went down the first nine floors in tremendous style and by the time we had got to number two I almost felt as if I was coming out of the Tattenham Corner in the Derby, lying fourth with a gap in front of me and Lester Piggott on top. But, for no good reason that I could see the lift now stopped. This put a completely different complexion on things.

With considerable alarm and foreboding I looked up, waiting for the light to come on. Sure enough, we had stopped at the top R. Before I could move, the lift doors juddered slightly and opened. Positively surging towards me were six ladies in long dresses and six men in dinner jackets, at the end of what had obviously been an excellent party.

I changed colour rapidly and probably as many as three times, going through the full range from red to puce, but my napkin stayed resolutely in position even if my hands were shaking a bit. The multitude advanced about two steps and three-quarters and then, seeing what lay ahead of them, stopped in amused horror.

They roared with laughter and there were screams of delight, which rapidly brought others to the lift door, and I was offered a great many gratuitous pieces of advice. I don't think I have ever felt so stupid, but I was saved after what seemed like half an hour but was probably only a few seconds by a short, bald-headed man. He came into the lift and said with a smile on his face, 'You look to be in a spot of bother.'

'How very quick of you to spot it,' I replied. Then I added as an after thought, 'The night porter's the chap I'm really after.' I could see immediately from the expression on his face that I could have rephrased this to advantage. However, he stood his ground in spite of the increasing clamour behind him (for I had rapidly become one of the sights of Nottingham), and told me that the night porter was, for some reason, just over there, and he pointed down the passage in a vague south-south-easterly direction.

He promised to fetch him and as he set off he said to me over his shoulder, 'Press the button which holds the door open.' I then had to perform a delicate operation which required perfect synchronisation if I was to get it right. While taking my hand off the right comer of the napkin to press the button at full stretch, I had simultaneously to move my left hand to the centre of the napkin if I was to remain even one tenth decent.

By a miracle I got it right too, to the intense disappointment of the considerable crowd. Before long, although it seemed like another year, a short, elderly night porter arrived, took one look at me and evidently did not care for what he saw. I told him what had happened. While he did not look too convinced he was at least prepared to help out. He came into the lift and pressed the button marked '9' and mercifully the doors shut.

But as I had pressed the bottom R in the first place, we continued to my abject horror on a downward path, but only for a short time as we came to a grinding halt at B. Some wag had run down the stairs and pressed the button on the outside. We stopped for long enough to see streams of people running from one floor to the next to have a look. There were more people at the bottom R, and I half expected the first of several air-conditioned coaches to arrive full to the brim with even more spectators.

The enthusiasm was so great that if anyone had charged a pound a look they would have made a killing. But the night porter kept his finger relentlessly down on the number nine button and the doors soon shut and we were on our way to safety -or so I thought. Of course, the jokers on the other floors had again pressed the buttons and so we made cursory stops at B and R where the splendid night porter, who was showing himself to be exactly the sort of chap you would like to have beside you in the trenches, repelled all potential boarders.

Believe it or not, we then went up the nine bedroom

floors without interruption. After the night porter had smiled, shaken his head a time or two and let me in with his pass key, I and my paper napkin were back in the sanctuary of my own room. The relief was so great that I had even forgotten that I wanted to spend a penny.

When I came down in the morning I was met by one of the managers who had already heard the story and found it hysterically funny. He then asked me why I had held the napkin where I had. I asked him what he meant.

'You see,' he began, 'most people are recognised by their faces. Wouldn't it have been more sensible to have held it in front of your face?'

JAIL BAIT

I know there have been times in my life which I would rather forget about or, at any rate, gloss over. This probably goes for all of us. I don't often catch myself looking back at this next story of when I was sent to prison in New York.

In almost every other situation I have got myself into, my overdeveloped sense of the ridiculous has nearly always saved me. There's always been something I've found that I could laugh at. You know, someone looks like Groucho Marx or talks like Peter Sellers or Peter Ustinov, a guy tells a funny story or something absurd happens or the situation seems quite unreal - which this one did but not in quite that way. As you will see, this was perhaps the only time in my life when my sense of humour and I went in diametrically opposite directions.

To start with I was hopelessly, or maybe helplessly, befuddled with booze - an excellent claret followed by some pretty decent cognac had been the cause that night- and therefore it was self inflicted to a great extent. At first I obeyed instructions as if in a mildly bad dream. Then as I sobered up which, as you will shortly see was swiftly to happen, the night assumed horrendous and nightmarish proportions. Therefore if in the next few pages you detect a certain clinical chill in my writing, well, I bet you wouldn't have enjoyed it either, for you will appreciate that it was a good deal less than comedy material. Even now as I read it through, the spectre of each and every moment rises most ingloriously in front of my eyes. Anyway here goes.

In November 1980, I flew into New York with a lovely girl I intended to marry. We were going to spend two or three days in Manhattan before disappearing into the mid-West. On our second night in New York we had been to a dinner party at an excellent restaurant with some friends of hers. One of those present was a chap who had played a considerable part in Cleo's life.

Live-in lover or surrogate husband, confidante and adviser and now, after her recent divorce, my leading rival. And as far as I could see that night he was about twelve lengths clear of the field and going away fast.

Altogether, I found it an evening which had singularly little to recommend it. I had, needless to say, drunk copiously throughout. When we ultimately returned to the confines of our hotel room, I felt that the whole of life was about 100 to 8 against and going further out by the second.

When neither apologies nor explanations were forthcoming, I felt that a certain amount of rough justice needed to be handed out. I then proceeded to make rather a hash of a bottom-smacking exercise which in my condition was not altogether surprising. Cleo, who was some way from seeing the funny side of it all, leapt out of bed, put on a coat and left the room in a hurry.

I returned to bed and about half an hour later was shaken out of a drunken half sleep by a furious beating on the door which could only have meant trouble. Dressed in a rather down-market pair of pants, I opened it just as more beating was beginning, to find half the New York police force outside with handcuffs in one hand and guns at the ready in the other.

I had been done for assault! So, under close security, I dressed, put my money and my passport into my pocket and held my hands together in front of me while they popped on a pair of handcuffs. This was another first.

I was taken down to the security offices of the hotel where the handcuffs were taken off and I was allowed to sit down while one of the policemen went off and told Cleo, in the next room, that they would see that I was moved to another hotel. But no, she did not feel that that was enough and so the night proceeded.

It was back on with the cuffs and I was walked across the large entrance hall in between two policemen and put into the back of a police car. One of the policemen sat beside me. They were both extremely friendly and sympathetic too, but told me that they could not take the law into their own hands. We drove to the neighbouring police station where they belonged.

I was now finger-printed to death. I had to dip each finger five times into a bowl of inky liquid and each time to press it firmly down onto a piece of paper. When that was done, I had to put the whole lot in together to do the full spread of the hand.

They then gave me considerable encouragement by telling me that I was in for a pretty torrid night. They told me I would be with a lot of blacks and it was important I should keep myself to myself. They asked me if I had any money on me and I produced getting on for three thousand dollars in cash and travellers' cheques.

They suggested I took off one of my shoes and the sock and put the money under my foot next to the skin. I produced my passport next and that went into my Y-fronts. I was still full of booze and I didn't even begin to appreciate what was in store for me. In a way I felt as if I was watching myself in a film. It was all very unreal as the handcuffs were put back on and we returned to the police car.

Again I sat in the back with a policeman and after about fifteen minutes we arrived at what I later discovered was the outpatients' department at the Tombs which, as far as I could see, was a conspicuously unfriendly downtown New York prison. I was taken from the car into a huge, bare, open room with a boarded floor. There were benches at intervals around the walls and I was told to sit down on one and my handcuffs were removed by the policeman who had brought me along.

He then said farewell to me and wished me a slightly chilling good luck; he said he would see me in court at eight o'clock in the morning. I don't think even then I was fully aware that I had had it and was going to spend the night in the nick.

There were about eight or ten other guys sitting around the walls. They were all Puerto Ricans and none of them seemed to be anticipating what lay ahead with any enthusiasm. After about twenty minutes something that sounded approximately like my name was shouted and I was told to go and stand in front of one of several grills.

I was faced by a tough-looking guy with a crew cut and glasses who had a pen at the ready. He asked me a series of questions in a voice which made it clear he reckoned I was amongst the scum of the earth. I answered as best I could, telling him why I was in New York and what I intended to do next.

When he had finished with me, a bruiser in jeans came through the door on my left and told me to follow him. It was another voice which brooked no argument, and I noticed a large bunch of keys hanging down on a chain almost to his knee.

We went through a passage into a much smaller room, with a desk full of papers in the middle and a chair behind it and an electric fire on the floor. He told me I could make one telephone call and pointed to a scruffy looking instrument on the comer of the desk.

I had a great friend in New York who I felt sure would be there and I put a call through to him. My luck was not in that night for there was no reply. I was about to dial another number when I was told that I had had my one call and if there was no answer it was tough titty. Which I didn't think was playing the game at all.

He now ordered me to empty my pockets. He put all the bits and pieces into an envelope and then told me to follow him. We went out of another door. As I went through I could smell the tension and also a nauseating stench of unwashed human beings. It was another large room and set in the middle were twenty iron prison cells painted a harsh yellow.

The cells were small, about ten feet across and twenty long. The front of each was barred and there were prisoners clutching these bars and shouting at the jailers. The light was dim although I could see that the cells were in two rows of ten, back to back. I felt I was living a nightmare as I grimly followed my guide, but now at last I knew my fate.

My chap busied himself when we got in front of the first cell by telling those who were shouting to shut their fucking mouths and then for good measure he called them mother fuckers. His language, I was to discover as the night went on, was obviously obligatory for a jailer when talking to a prisoner.

He stopped in front of the fourth cell, threw open the door with a terrifying flourish and there was a sickening finality about the rattle of his keys. He pushed me into the semi-dark, evil-smelling interior saying, 'You'll be spending the night with these gentlemen.' Now I don't imagine you're ever allowed to choose your cell mates in this type of situation, but just supposing you were, my first glance told me that the lot who faced me would not have been at the top of anyone's list.

I was scared rigid as I walked into that cell. If I still needed anything to sober me up, it was the final, chilling clang as he shut the door and turned the key. It produced a dreadful feeling of hopelessness.

Immediately on the right was a small bench which folded back against the wall. A couple of junkies were slumped on it and they were taking less than a nominal interest in life. Against the back wall on either side of a lavatory pan which, judging by the mess and the smell, was blocked up, were three more prisoners who stared at me through sullen, hostile eyes which unnerved me even more. The light was not good but even so the mood of my companions was not difficult to detect.

I was told the next morning by one jailer that I was the only white man among 160 holding prisoners that night. They were a mixture of junkies, transvestites, car thieves, burglars, petty criminals and drunks. He told me that many of them probably had three or four other charges outstanding against them. There was not one I would have chosen as a running mate.

I stood quite still by the wall on my left quite close to the barred door. The stench was awful and the atmosphere was eerie beyond belief. The silence was constantly broken by yells from other cells as prisoners called to each other or yelled to the jailers to come and light their cigarettes. We were not allowed to have our own matches. Junkies who were showing withdrawal symptoms kept yelling that they wanted to go to hospital. There was also the incoherent babbling of drunks. It was blood curdling.

For some time I was watched by the three at the back of the cell who occasionally spoke amongst themselves in low voices. Then, they came towards me. Not knowing what was happening I stayed where I was and when they were a few steps away, the biggest began to throw a punch.

I automatically brought up my arms to defend my face and as I did so one of the other two kicked me hard in the balls with shattering accuracy. I fell down on the floor, whereupon they attacked me, kicking and punching and trying to go through my pockets. It was painful and after one nasty crack on the side of the head I began to wonder if I would ever get out alive. When it was followed by another I began to shout with pain.

This sent my assailants running like rats to the back wall. It also produced a jailer who, as he came through the door from the office, gave a loud, 'What the fuck's happening?' When he saw me he called me a mother fucker, asked me why the fuck I thought I was there in the first place and after a few more throat-clearing oaths went back through the door to the office, ignoring requests for matches or hospitals or drinks.

Nothing happened for another twenty minutes. Then the three approached me again and it obviously was not a friendly visit. I stood my ground but soon they were grappling with me. By way of variation or maybe simply to teach me a lesson for getting the jailer,

two held me down while the other pissed all over me and then they took it in turn.

Then, one of them spotted my signet ring which he clearly thought was a legitimate spoil. He found he was unable to pull it off and set about trying to twist my finger off. Again I yelled in pain and protested and while my friends fled, the jailer was quickly through the door reeling off a few more well-chosen epithets as he came.

But to my immense relief, he unlocked the door and half dragged me out into the passage before shoving me into another cell about four along the row. By then, I was feeling almost indecently sorry for myself.

I had six cell mates this time and I watched them from just inside the door with considerable foreboding while they stared back at me, I feared, in eager anticipation. The policemen were right; it was not being a pleasant evening.

I stood still trying to make myself appear as small and insignificant as possible. Once or twice one of them moved, but mercifully nothing happened although I spent the night, terrified, standing on one foot and then the other. I have never known time pass so slowly and I still could not believe that all this was in fact happening to me. I well remember thinking soon after I arrived in my new cell that maybe it was to prepare me for eventualities of this sort that my parents had spent a small fortune on my education at Eton and Cambridge, but in the circumstances the thought raised not even a faint smile.

Every time the telephone rang on the jailer's desk - I could easily hear it through the door - I was sure that it was someone ringing up to say that it had all been a hideous mistake. Of course, the call never came. Dawn broke, but nothing happened. Eight o'clock, when my policeman had told me that he would see me in court, came and went.

There were still the hysterical yells from those wanting a light for their cigarettes, or to go to hospital - for the withdrawal symptoms were biting sharper by now. And there were some who wanted to know when they were going to court. Others wanted food which they were most certainly not going to get for they were told in ringing tones by the jailers to 'shut your fucking mouths'.

Eventually at about eleven o'clock, the first ones to go to court were taken away. Their names were called and when each one answered he was taken out of the cell and made to stand in front. They stood in lots of four in line ahead formation and each had a handcuff, which was attached to the same long chain, locked on their right hand wrist.

It was the afternoon before my name was called. They clearly thought I was good officer material for I was put in the front of my four with a couple of junkies and a drunk bringing up the rear. It took an age to get them all to face the same way so that the handcuffs could be applied. Then, we were put back into an empty cell and soon we were joined by four more who included three transvestites who smelled of a mixture of cheap scent and shit.

The transvestites wanted to race off everything in sight and most particularly me as far as I could see and it was not the happiest hour I have ever spent. Then, at last, it was time to go. We were led out through various passages to a courtyard at the back of the prison and were told to climb into the back of a van. Being chained together, it required a certain mutual co-ordination which was not always forthcoming.

We were crammed into the van like sardines and had a most uncomfortable drive to a court which sat seven days a week. When we arrived the police took over and I was made with the others to put the palms of my hands above my head against the wall while I was frisked. I was then told to take off my shoes and one of them felt under my feet and located my money. I had to produce it and it was held up to the assembled company. The look in their eyes was not encouraging.

I was then put into a cramped holding cell where there were about fifty people and now that my money was known about I thought that I had had it even though the handcuffs had been taken off. Suddenly, I heard someone shout my name. I looked around and it was the policeman who had arrested me and who had said that he would see me in court.

I was taken out of the cell and the policeman told me that he had managed to persuade those in charge to bring me forward. He had done so because if I had stayed where I was the chances of my having to spend another night in the cells were high because there was a considerable backlog of prisoners. From then on my mind was obsessed with the possibility of having to spend another night like that. It was almost too ghastly to contemplate.

I was put into a smaller cell where I stood around while legal aid attorneys continually shouted the names of the prisoners whom they were going to act for. When a prisoner's name had been called he went into a small cubicle to confer through a grill with the lawyer. One or two were told that without doubt they would be held in prison and later given a prison sentence. It did not appear unduly to worry them.

When my turn came I had a nice young lawyer who told me that I would be discharged for it was not a serious charge and he did not imagine anyone would turn up to give evidence against me.

The next time my name was called, it was to go down the passage into the large Victorian courtroom. I went in with my policeman through a door at the side of the magistrate's bench and we sat on a wooden stool awaiting our turn. Justice was being dispensed at a fair speed and soon I was next in line.

But as soon as the case in front of me had finished, the magistrate announced that there would be a break in proceedings. Until business was resumed I was taken back to the cell. By this time I had some more cigarettes which the policeman had bought for me.

I rationed myself to one every twenty minutes and after I had smoked three of them I was called again, but now there were two prisoners in front of me, for they had their own private lawyers and so were allowed to queue jump.

Then, at last I was standing in front of the magistrate having been told by my lawyer not to open my mouth at any stage. His opposite number was a girl and it was quickly agreed that as I was on my way to Australia I should be allowed to depart. I was told that if I kept the peace for six months all records would be destroyed.

That was that and I walked down the full length of the packed courtroom, out of the double doors, down the steps and into the fresh air. I was a free man and it was over. I took my friendly policeman to a pub for a glass of beer before taking a taxi back to my hotel to pick up my bags.

Rather furtively, I explained to the bell captain who I was. He looked down at me as if I was something the cat had brought in which was more than unusually unpleasant, or at any rate as if I was part of the castle not normally shown to visitors. Trying to avoid my eyes, he told me as impersonally as he could that my bags would be brought down.

While I waited I suddenly saw Cleo's bags by the desk and I looked round and there she was about twenty paces away. I walked towards her and said, 'Hi, Cleo.' As I did a hand gripped my elbow from behind and a huge black bouncer growled at me as he pushed me away, 'Be on your way mister.'

They had been eighteen unforgettable hours.

AFTER HOURS

I made a pretty unconventional start to my first tour of Australia when I flew into Perth in October 1968 to watch a series against the West Indies. After one jet-lagged night in the Rhodes Motel, I found myself aboard a sleeper heading for the famous old mining town of Kalgoorlie where the West Indies were to play their first match against a country eleven.

The train set off in the early evening and I spent much of the journey in the highly agreeable company of two Australian cricket writers, Keith Butler from Adelaide and Phil Tresidder from Sydney. But my first discovery on climbing aboard came as a bit of a shock. The train had a restaurant car, but the bar, like all others in Western Australia on a Sunday, was irrevocably shut.

There were no flies on Keith, however, and with a knowing smile he patted a cardboard box on the seat beside him when I complained. It was full of cans of beer. Having solved that problem we tested the dining car and dinner, served by a Pommie student, consisted of a large plate of corned beef hash out of a tin and it was certainly very hot.

Looking back on that journey now, reminds me of a story of the famous English cricket writer Jim Swanton on one of his last tours of Australia when he decided to travel from Sydney to Perth by train.

Soon after joining the train in Sydney he wandered down to the bar where he asked for a pink gin which the barman obligingly mixed for him . During the night the train crossed the border between New South Wales and Victoria and a Victorian crew took over.

The next day before lunch Swanton returned to the bar and asked the new barman, a rather solid, foursquare individual, if he would mind making him a pink gin. He was a trifle startled by the reply given in ringing tones, 'Mate, we only keep white fuckin' gin on this ship.'

Kalgoorlie the next morning was straight out of a Western. It was a glorious day, the streets were wide and dusty, every second house was a pub with those half-hack swinging doors and the hats of those going in, if not ten gallons, were a good half dozen. John Wayne was always likely to be the next man in.

We stayed in the main hotel which I am sure was called the Palace and it was a splendidly impressive building in its dark Victorian and rather stately way although I doubt if it had seen too many coats of paint since World War I.

When the England side had visited Kalgoorlie at the start of the 1962/63 tour with the Earl Marshall, the Duke of Norfolk, as its manager, the bedrooms had no basins. As a result all those present had a jolly get together every morning in the communal shaving area. The Duke was always there, but apparently he never cut himself and they were not able to find out how blue his blood actually was.

The West Indies match was a two-day affair and after dinner at the hotel on the first evening - as a special concession the time for last orders had been stretched from 6:30 to 7:00 - several of us went for a walk and ended up for a glass of beer in the main street at Hannan's Hotel.

Hannan is a famous name in Kalgoorlie for the first nugget of gold was found there towards the end of the last century by an Irishman called Paddy Hannan. There is Hannan's Street and Hannan's Hotel and Hannan's Memorial and Hannan's everything else.

The hotel had a large bar which was packed for it was a favourite meeting place for the miners who had given the bar its tough, no-nonsense atmosphere. Our group consisted of five for in addition to Keith Butler and Phil Tresidder, there was Peter Loader, the old England fast bowler who lived in Perth and who was, among many other things, a cricket commentator. The fifth member was a Dutch technician from the ABC who for the duration of this trip was known as Feedback. He had flown up from Perth with the commentators early that morning and when the pilot made one announcement over the Tannoy there was a good deal of interference. Feedback had shaken his head knowingly and had muttered, 'Feedback', and so Feedback it was.

Later we were joined by the cartoonist Paul Rigby who was then working for one of Rupert Murdoch's papers in Perth, and Bernie Kirwan Ward, an Englishman who wrote a column under Rigby's cartoon on the back page. Since then, Rigby, who is one of the world's more extravagant and delightful extroverts, has acquired considerable fame from his cartoons for Murdoch's papers in Sydney, London and New York.

That evening in Hannan's I received my first lesson in Australian beer drinking habits. We were all drinking beer and being Australian beer it was a new experience for me. Unlike the lukewarm pints and half pints served in English pubs, Australian beer is always ice cold and in my book preferable to English beer. Of course, with the possible exception of 'bodyline', there is no more contentious subject when Australians and Poms get together than the respective merits of their beer.

My only problem with Australian beer is that because it is so cold I find it difficult to drink fast because it hurts the back of my throat. That first night I was going very slowly and soon found that I was being lapped by most of those I was drinking with. While I sipped away at the glass in my hand a line of three more full ones was sitting on the bar awaiting my attention.

By then, a group of miners had joined us and one of them, a massive chap with forearms like a couple of oak trees, brandished a purple five-dollar bill and ordered another round. I must have looked a trifle apprehensive and he watched me closely as I lifted my glass to my lips for another taste.

He then exploded, 'Jesus, mate, drink the stuff, don't fuckin' sip it.'

They drank and I sipped on until just after midnight when Rigby looked at his watch.

'They'll be closed now, it's after twelve o'clock. We'll go and pay a social visit to the girls I know in one of the drums in Hay Street, which is that street there,' he said for my benefit, pointing at the back door. He then explained to me that the drums are legalised brothels which cater for the needs of the miners.

The wooden houses or drums all have raised verandahs and the ladies sit outside in their finery, showing off their wares. That way the miners can easily see the menu as they drive slowly by and can stop and order accordingly. The brothels are staffed by girls who, on the journey from Sydney or wherever, have acquired foreign names and broken English accents.

Their activities are controlled by the police and business hours end sharp at midnight. I was told that the drums are one of the reasons there is so little crime in Kalgoorlie. Frequent medical inspections are also compulsory.

On an earlier visit to Kalgoorlie, Rigby had been taken on a social visit to one of the drums and had been given an open invitation to return whenever he was there. Five of us (Tresidder and Kirwan Ward had opted out) set off along the garden path at the back of Hannan's and out through the rickety wooden gate into Hay Street where there was no longer much activity. A couple of sporting combatants who had arrived just before twelve o'clock for a quickie were driving off.

The drums, there must have been at least ten, still had their lights on and led by Rigby, we turned left out of the gate, although for a moment or two he was not sure where he was heading. Then it came to him and we set off down the street and when we had gone a hundred yards or so, there came an excited female shriek of 'Rigby!' from the other side of the road.

They had found us. Considering the time and our non-operational intentions our greeting was stupendous. There were three girls led by an ebullient, bouncy and booby blonde and also there was the austere madame who supervised this particular drum.

I shall always remember her for she had the most extraordinarily wrinkled face I have ever seen and, although she knew Rigby, it was still tinged with a fair amount of suspicion. I dare say she had been there a long time and when her own operational days on the shop floor had ended, she had gone over to management and was always on the lookout for sharp practice.

As soon as we were sitting down inside a rather narrow sitting room with bedrooms opening off it all over the place, Rigby, with great pomp and ceremony, introduced us to the girls. First, Keith Butler, who was permanently wreathed in smiles, was introduced as Emile de Something-or-other, the famous French fashion designer who, to substantiate this, immediately seized hold of the nearest hem saying as he did so, 'That's a lovely piece of stuff,' in an accent which was marginally more Adelaidian than Parisian.

The girls were confident that Peter Loader was Bernie Kirwan Ward and so that was who he became. Feedback was Feedback who for reasons of security could not use his proper name. Finally, Rigby went into a long speech about the British aristocracy before introducing me as Lord Henry Fitz-Counterpipe - I never knew whether or not I really had a hyphen - the dissolute younger son of a Duke.

After that, conversation went along at a furious pace while the girls produced vast quantities of rum and coke and thanked us with tears in their eyes for bringing some culture into their humdrum lives. One after the other they disappeared and returned with their entire wardrobe on their arms for Emile to run his eye over.

'Lovely piece of stuff,' he kept on saying, occasionally interspersed with a I'll bet that was made in Paris.' And the girl in question made a mental note to snip off the 'Made in Australia' label when she got back to her room.

The big blonde then told Rigby that this particular drum was faced with a nasty problem. A year before one of the drums up the road had had a birthday party and had acquired the services of a five-piece band which had kept going until dawn and had given the drum great fame. Then, two or three weeks before our visit, the drum opposite had also had a birthday party and they had got hold of a much bigger band which had second violinists stretching halfway down Hay Street.

Now, in a week's time our drum was having a birthday party and so far they had been unable to find a band with a single second violinist and they were in despair for they felt their social standing would take a knock. All eyes turned to Rigby who rubbed his massive chin thoughtfully, said he felt sure that he would come up with a solution, while Emile tweaked another hemline and said with great authority, 'What a lovely piece of stuff.'

Without saying anything, Rigby got up and went out

of the room, apparently following directions to the loo. We went on talking and he did not come back for nearly half an hour and when he then appeared he asked the booby blonde to come and have a look at something.

There were wild shrieks of joy from the biggest bedroom and the blonde burst back into the sitting room grinning from ear to ear and insisted we all came and had a look. We followed her back and on the large wall opposite the double bed was a remarkable cartoon Rigby had just drawn.

In the foreground was a large bed and on it lay a copulating couple. Behind them and stretching away to the right and left was the biggest band you have ever seen in your life. It was filled to the brim with third trombonists, it was bristling with fourth cellists and you could hardly see yourself for second violinists. No customer had ever brought such yells of contentment, jubilation and satisfaction to this drum, especially with his trousers still on, as Rigby had done now. It enabled them to win the Great Band Contest, game, set and match.

While I was in the bedroom I found myself standing next to a big wickerwork laundry basket in the comer. In the crush I was pushed against it and the lid came partly off. I saw that the basket was stuffed almost to the top with twenty dollar bills. Business was good and those were the days when twenty dollars were more like twenty dollars than they are today.

Back in the sitting room we were exhorted to attack new and stronger rums and Cokes when suddenly I heard Rigby telling the madame in solemn tones that never before had this drum been honoured by such an aristocratic visitor as Lord Henry Fitz-Counterpipe. He went on to suggest that it was important that the girls or at least one of them should do the decent thing to mark the occasion.

I thought the booby blonde was entering fully into the spirit of things when she engineered me without any great difficulty into another bedroom. But once the door was shut she showed that this was no amateur lark-about and demanded the full twenty dollars which

I though was a bit thick.

I spoke to her about her unchristian attitude and outlook but she remained resolute and, as much as I tried, was not even prepared to negotiate. With a final shrug of her shoulders which sent her boobs into mad bouncing vibrations, she opened the door and left the room.

Peter Loader told me afterwards, and never stops telling me still whenever I see him, that the party in the sitting room were sent into convulsions when at one point my voice came booming through the wall saying rather huffily, 'But you don't understand, it takes me at least an hour to make love'. Talk about whistling to keep your courage up.

Not long after this we said our goodbyes and left. The girls, with one exception as far as I was concerned, were tearfully happy and drunk and after a final, 'Lovely piece of stuff-ing' from Emile we tottered back to our different hotels. I began a short lie down before breakfast soon after five o'clock. I believe Rigby's cartoon is still there and has become one of Kalgoorlie's major tourist attractions. I wonder what has happened to the girls.

RIO AND ALL THAT

For most of us there are, I think, parts of the world which are remote, mystical and inaccessible and, maybe partly as a result, strangely alluring and incomparably fascinating. South America has always been the place for me and has seemed too beguiling for words. I never thought I had the slightest chance of getting there. I know that technically Guyana, part of the cricketing West Indies, is in South America, but it was Rio and Buenos Aires and Peru and the Pacific Coast that I was really after.

The miracle happened in 1978 when I was watching the New Zealanders play Derrick Robins Eleven at Eastbourne in the first match of their tour. I was talking to Derrick, who was a long-time friend, and he told me that he was taking a side of young County cricketers on a tour to five Latin American countries the following March. I told him how envious I was and he immediately said, 'Why don't you come, for goodness sake? Peter Parfitt [he batted for England in 37 Test matches] is going to manage the side and you can be his assistant.' I then did a certain amount of 'You don't really mean it do you-ing' and, wonderful to relate, it was clear that he did.

Late in February 1979, just after I had come back to England from covering Mike Brearley's first tour of Australia (1978/79), the Derrick Robins Eleven and officials gathered for lunch in the Cricketers Club of London, Frank Russell's admirable establishment in Blandford Street. We were issued with our tour kit of ties, caps, tracksuits, shirts, sweaters and even a do-it-yourself medical box which had some exhilarating contents although happily I never had to bring mine into action. After lunch we drove to London Airport and flew off to Madrid. There we picked up an Iberian Airlines Jumbo and off we went to Bogotá in Colombia by way of San Juan in Puerto Rico where we refuelled in easily the most uncomfortable international airport I have so far experienced.

On all the cricket tours I have been part of, I have never been as excited as I was at the start of this one. And, far from being let down, my expectations were greatly exceeded. It was a tremendous month.

The only thing I knew about Bogotá was that England's football captain, Bobby Moore, had been arrested there on a trumped up charge of stealing jewellery when England played a warm-up match there before the 1970 World Cup finals in Mexico. We landed early in the morning and were met by the interminable chaos of a totally disorganised airport. Small, darkhaired Colombians bristling with black moustaches were shouting furiously at one another, waving their arms like tic-tac men and generally making a meal of the macho bit. When they spoke to us or indeed to anyone else it was as if they were actively engaged in declaring the outbreak of World War III.

Eventually we emerged from the Customs, were met by our mainly expatriate hosts and were taken by car to our various billets. I found that I, along with Derrick himself and Kelly Seymour, our delightful doctor who had bowled his off breaks in seven Test matches for South Africa, had been given beds with His Excellency, the British Ambassador, which was nothing if not a promising start.

The Residence was charming, with a delightful walled garden. We lived and were looked after in some style. The Ambassador had recently finished a longish sojourn in Moscow and some conflicting views about communism were expressed. When the conversation turned to South Africa it all got very exciting and almost out of hand. The only slight problem about staying in diplomatic circles was that kidnapping ambassadors had become something of a national pastime in Bogotá and so H.E. had a permanent supply of bodyguards. They were tough-looking blokes I wouldn't have wanted to pick an argument with and they all had the telltale bulges under their coats. It was good honest James Bond stuff.

Driving in Bogotá was an immensely hazardous pursuit and you did not have to be an ambassador to suffer. Everyone drove flat out with their hands on their horns. It was soon apparent that traffic signals were there simply for decorative purposes. It was essential to lock car doors from the inside and to keep windows shut at all times.

Pick-pocketing is a major industry. If a driver is careless enough to leave his window open, goodness only knows what the pedestrians will remove from the car and those inside it while it is stationary in a traffic jam. If a driver wears his watch on his left wrist and rests his arm on the door with the window open, it is the work of a moment for a passing pedestrian to nick it off his wrist. Small children are trained as pick-pockets. They make the chap who removes your wallet, tie and braces at a circus without you feeling a thing look like the answer to question one. If there was a pick-pocketing competition at the Olympic Games, Colombia would win the gold medal unchallenged.

We were in Bogotá for two nights and did not therefore have much of a chance to do more than to drive round the city and look at the old Spanish buildings from the outside, although I was taken up to the mountains which overlooks the city and from where there was the most perfect view. I also visited the embassy with H.E. and we went in through a secret entrance which is there to bamboozle any potential kidnappers. Even in the short space of our stay I was made acutely aware that the law of the jungle applied rather too closely for comfort. We also had a delightful day's cricket on a charmingly rural ground in the shadow of the mountains and we beat a side made up of nationals from many cricket playing countries, including an old West Indian Test player, W. A. White, who played two matches against Australia in 1964.

We then flew on to Lima in Peru where the exchange rate made life fairly cheap for foreigners while rampant inflation had put most of the high spots out of bounds for the locals. In the three days we were there, I made friends with one or two beguilingly beautiful dark-haired Peruvian girls whose intentions turned out to be considerably more chaste than they had originally led us to believe. Most disappointing.

Everywhere we went in South America I was amazed at the former size and influence of the British communities. One illustration of this was the way in which the British still owned prime real estate in the middle of the cities. On the open market the land would have realised a fortune. The British still used it for the pleasure of playing cricket. In Lima, the Cricket and Tennis Club was a perfect example. There was a good-sized cricket field, a big club house and a separate English style pub. There, cricket was played once or twice a week and the only local interest in the club concerned the tennis courts which were packed with Peruvians. It was the same in Santiago, Buenos Aires and Rio.

Lima was tremendous fun until the very end and even that was the fault of the Chileans rather than the Peruvians. When the day came to leave, we all went to the airport only to find that the flight to Santiago on Varig, the Chilean airline, had been overbooked. Although we had reconfirmed reservations, and any amount of Latin-American waving of arms went on, two of us had to remain behind.

It's always as well to have an assistant manager because in these circumstances he is an ideal chap to leave behind. One of the players was deputed to stay with me and we were driven back into Lima to the Hotel Bolivar. By the time we got there I had begun to feel decidedly unwell.

I went straight to bed in one of those old high-ceilinged rooms in an elderly hotel and two hours later my temperature had gone past 105. The hotel rallied round and produced the most villainous looking doctor it has ever been my lot to see, although he had an undoubted twinkle in his eye.

He was macho to the eyebrows. With considerable glee he announced that he was going to give me an injection and so I told him that I was allergic to penicillin. He did not seem as impressed by this piece of information as I would have liked him to be. He kept on grinning and assuring me that everything would be all right. With that, he pulled out from his bag one of the most venomous looking needles I have ever seen and a phial of colourless liquid. With great relish he drew up the injection.

It was at this point I panicked for I could now see my life ending in a sweat-filled bed in Lima, which was not at all how I had planned it. I snatched the telephone and, miraculously, I did not have to wait long before I got hold of the manager who spoke English. He agreed to come up.

I tried to engage the doctor in light conversation to delay the jab until the manager arrived and mercifully I succeeded. The manager soon burst into the room, also full of smiles. I told him that it was a matter of considerable urgency that he should impress upon my friend, the doctor, that I was badly allergic to penicillin. The two of them then had an animated conversation which went on at a fierce pace for about three minutes. I began to think they were agreeing to fix me once and for all.

Anyway, when it had finished, the doctor brought

out another phial from his bag and with a joy which had not subsided one iota he prepared another injection. Then, with a triumphant glint in his eye, he advanced on me holding the instrument as if it was a bayonet on the end of a rifle. He told me to bend over and under the close scrutiny of the manager he thrust

the needle into my arse, squirted the stuff in, pulled the needle out with a flourish, gave me some pills, and exacted an exorbitant fee for his efforts.

He assured me I would be fit to fly the next morning and then, with gales of laughter, he and the manager left me to get on with it. I shall never know how close an escape I had, but whatever he gave me did the trick and the next morning, after a great struggle to get two seats, I was on the aeroplane heading for Chile.

I would have loved to have spent longer than two days in Santiago which I found the most delightful city. We also had two nights in Sao Paulo, a massive industrial city in inland Brazil.

And then it was on to Rio. There cannot possibly be another city in the world in such a dramatically beautiful setting, although Sydney is not all that far behind. They both have magnificent harbours but for my money the mountain overlooking Rio gives it the edge.

The huge white figure of Christ, the Corcovado, high on the mountain behind the city looking out over the water is as spectacular as anything I have ever seen. The view looking down on Rio, its waterways and the surrounding sea and country, is equally stunning.

In a week we did little more than the conventional tourist bit, but even so I came away feeling that the dramatic physical beauty of the place did not go far below the surface. For four days we drove across the bridge over the harbour, which is several miles long and said to be the longest in the world, to the lovely suburb of Niteroi where we played cricket on another lovely ground.

We spent a day on a motor cruiser which belonged

to British American Tobacco, going round the harbour and lunching on a remote beach. And needless to say, the expensive red light district on the Copacabana was systematically explored. More especially, we were introduced to the quite unforgettable charms of a club called the New Munich.

Each evening in a small room twelve of the most perfect, dark-haired Brazilian ladies performed on the stage the gentle and progressively less gentle exhibition of the arts of lesbianism. It was exquisitely beautiful, enormously whole-hearted – I could vouch for this for I was squashed up against the stage with my knee just over the top and several times it was squeezed tightly by one combatant in an ecstasy which had nothing to do with me. Yes, it was an evening to remember all right.

Some days later we flew back to London, each one of us with our own special memories of our South American journey.

CURRIED AWAY

I am often amazed by the average Westerner's view of India. They seem to presume that every night is spent in a black hole of Calcutta, that every glass of water produces typhoid, not to mention cholera, that amoebic dysentery is an almost obligatory companion and that, if there is anything else left to go wrong, the food will fix it in a matter of moments.

I find this irritating for not only is it untrue, but also India is one of the most fascinating countries of all to visit in terms of both the present and the past. In the cities especially, the hotels are excellent, water out of the tap has never hurt me, the food is delicious, the people are different but quite charming and there is so much to see. I always look forward to India.

Having said that, travellers to India must not make the cardinal mistake of comparing it to the West. The meanest intelligence must surely understand that before first leaving home. More than six hundred million people, intense poverty and a civilisation based largely on the Hindu religion have combined to produce a way of life which is a million light years away from that in the suburbs of any Western city.

The Indian temperament also takes a little getting used to. The timelessness which is inherent in all of life in the East needs to be absorbed. The spectacle of angry Europeans shouting and screaming at an Indian who barely understands English, although eager to please, is as embarrassing as their behaviour is stupid and futile. Of course, I have been guilty of behaving like this at times. All it succeeds in doing is ensuring that the process, whatever it is, takes even longer.

I have often caught a taxi outside the Taj Mahal Hotel in Bombay and have asked one of those splendid looking chaps in their purple turbans who preside over events in the courtyard to tell the driver my destination. We start off and gradually it becomes apparent that the driver has not the faintest idea of where I am heading for. It's a difficult moment, for he with the best will in the world cannot understand English and I cannot speak a word of his language. Eventually a pedestrian is found who speaks English and who tells the driver the address. The driver then reveals that he does not know where the street is. And so it goes on.

I had an interesting experience in Bombay when I tried to collect, in rupees, some money I was owed in order to spend it in the same city. The year before when a similar situation had arisen, I had been taken to the State Bank of India where my account was held and after a delightful chat with my bank manager who was the former Indian captain, Ajit Wadekar, I collected 40,000 rupees.

When I tried again this time I was hoping to get hold of 50,000 rupees. I was picked up at the Taj Mahal one morning by Mr Raj, who worked for the same group of newspapers. Off we went by taxi, full of smiles and confidence, to the State Bank of India. Ajit Wadekar had been moved to another branch and the first deskbound official we encountered shunted us down to the basement where, in fairly crowded conditions, rather bigger brass conducted their business. Mr Raj had all the relevant papers and while we sat down behind a desk he spoke to the charming official sitting behind it. In typical Indian fashion much nodding of heads ensued.

It is difficult if you don't speak the language to tell quite which way the conversation is going, but for some time I felt confident that I was winning. It was bound

to take time and I kept completely quiet throughout the long conversation. Then the Charming Official got up and walked over and had a long conversation with an older and more austere colleague whose desk was behind Mr Raj and myself.

I realised at once from the tone of this new conversation that I had gone right back in the betting. The Austere Colleague appeared to be adamant that I would not be able to get my money. He then sent the Charming Official across the room to find the huge tome which contained the regulations governing foreign exchange control in India.

The Austere Colleague, who was wearing a green shirt, now thumbed interminably through the pages. By now, I was resigned to the timeless process which had taken over. Mr Raj was not so relaxed for he was, I think, embarrassed that I was being held up like this.

The Charming Official now returned to his desk and told Mr Raj that the problem was that I had 55,000 rupees in my account. Foreign Exchange regulations stated that if a foreigner has a balance of more than 50,000 rupees in his account he could not withdraw more than 10,000 in any one year.

As it so happened, when I had taken out 40,000 the previous year, the balance had been 49,750 rupees. I immediately suggested that I should withdraw 10,000 there and then and come back the next day for 40,000, for then my balance would be less than 50,000. This produced masses of head shaking and tongue clicking but ultimately no joy.

Mr Raj now sat down in front of the Austere Colleague's desk and had a long conversation in which Ajit Wadekar's name was repeatedly mentioned. Ajit was now the manager of a branch out near the airport and he was playing cricket that day for his branch in an interbank competition. Mr Raj came over to me and told me that we had to go to the ground and see him and so we got a taxi and set off to one of the maidans near the Gymkhana Ground.

There were a great many games being played and it took us a while to locate Ajit's. Naturally, he was in the field. Seeing him bending down at first slip dampened my spirits as the lunch interval was still sometime off. No sooner had we reached the wooden pavilion than we were joined by a smiling official who had been watching and who was eager to help.

He was obviously of some importance in the bank. At once he gave the twelfth man a message to take out to Ajit at the end of the over. Ajit gratefully took the chance of a few minutes rest, for it was extremely hot and he was drowning in sweat. After demolishing a soft drink and lighting a cigarette, he assured me that I would have no trouble collecting my money and told the Smiling Official to tell someone at the bank that I was a good friend of his.

Soon Mr Raj and I and the Smiling Official were in a taxi heading back to the State Bank of India. We went up the entrance stairs and straight to the lift which after a spot of hissing and gurgling went slowly up one floor. We walked down the corridor until right at the end there were some chairs outside an impressive looking door.

It was the Managing Director's office and after we had sat down on the chairs, the Smiling Official wrote a note which he gave to the man on the door guarding the entrance. Almost immediately we were asked to go in. The Boss was extremely friendly behind his horn-rimmed glasses. He soon suggested that the three of us should go upstairs to his private dining room and have lunch while he tried to find a way through the regulations.

We walked up one flight of stairs into a big, rather dark dining room with a huge round polished table in the middle. Miraculously, an army of servants produced a delicious four-course lunch after being given about five minutes' notice. We then returned to the Boss's office and he told us he had found a way round my problem and all would be well. The regulations said that foreign journalists could be paid as long as their payment did not exceed $50 an article. Smiles all round and much handshaking for we had kicked it. I was paid $30 an article.

It was now back to the basement for the Smiling Official, Mr Raj and myself. Once again I found myself sitting in front of the Austere Colleague's desk. For some reason the all-pervading air of bonhomie upstairs had not filtered through to the basement. More long discussions were entered into and the Austere Colleague was still looking particularly austere. At this point our little expedition to cash a cheque so that I could spend my own money right there in Bombay had been going on for more than four hours.

It later transpired that a newfound technical problem had prompted the Boss to ring down to the Austere Colleague while the three of us had been in transit between his office and the basement. The Boss had said that payment must be withheld. Mr Raj assured me that the Austere Colleague was doing all he could to help and at one stage he even wrote out the form authorising payment which I had signed in two places.

He made one more telephone to the Boss, but met with another massive negative whereupon he tore the form into small pieces. Amid a positive orgy of nodding and a mass of sympathetic smiles we agreed to resume the battle the next day at 9:30 in the morning. By then Mr Raj promised to have the evidence that each payment was well within the rules.

On the way back to the Taj Mahal Hotel Mr Raj assured me that the visit the next morning would be nothing more than a formality and I would have the rest of the day to spend my money. Even so, I could not help feeling that earning it was much easier than collecting it.

At 9:20 a.m. Mr Raj picked me up and back we went to the basement of the State Bank of India and the Austere Colleague. With the air of one who had been dealt the joker at last, Mr Raj handed the Austere Colleague some papers on which he had neatly typed the number of articles I had written and the amount I had been paid month by month. For example, in one month I had written 13 articles and had been paid 3,900 rupees at 300 rupees or $30.00 per piece.

The Austere Colleague studied the papers for a long time and then spoke to Mr Raj. I could tell at once that we were still some way from winning. The problem now appeared to be that I was paid 3,900 rupees in one cheque and not 13 individual cheques of 300 rupees each which was apparently what the regulations stated.

This was clearly an insuperable problem. Anyway, after more discussions between Mr Raj and the Austere Colleague, we set off again for the Boss's office. Again, we sat down outside and a note was sent in. We were soon allowed in too and while the others sat down, I remained standing. My sense of humour was fast beginning to run out.

Mr Raj again proffered his letter and the Boss said it was not good enough. The chances of picking up my cash now seemed to be precisely zero. Stupidly, I now intervened and stepping up to the desk I told the Boss that surely any fool could divide 13 into 3,900 whereupon he told me sharply that that was not the point for he could not possibly go against the regulations.

I told him that the process of trying to collect my own money to spend in India had taken nearly seven hours and complained bitterly. The Boss sharply rejected my complaints, nodded his head and dismissed us. In the passage outside the Austere Colleague and Mr Raj decided that they would make one final throw and go and see an official at the Reserve Bank of India which was nearby.

It was a five-minute walk and after asking questions in two huge, crowded offices in an elderly colonial building, we were shown to a rickety old lift which only held four people and took us to the fourth floor. Mr Raj was left behind as there was already someone in the lift and he would have made the fifth.

I was intrigued to see that the licence for the lift which was in a frame on the back wall had been originally made out in handwriting to the Maharajah of Wankaner. Sometime later a line had been drawn from the Maharajah's name to the margin where in more handwriting it said that the licence had subsequently been taken over by the Reserve Bank of

India. The ruling princes had been stripped of their titles back in the 1960s.

On the sixth floor the Austere Colleague and I were steered to a youngish man who sat behind a desk covered with piles of papers and books. The Austere Colleague stated our problem, and I did not need to be a genius to tell that the dialogue got off to a bad start. I was told that the maximum I could withdraw was 10,000 rupees and he added that he was not at all sure that my withdrawal of 40,000 rupees the year before had been in strict accordance with the laws.

In the meantime I had decided that it was now too late for me to take the money out in rupees for I no

longer had time to spend it; already it was half past twelve on a Saturday afternoon and I was leaving Bombay the following day. I had also decided that in the future it would be best if I was paid direct in pounds sterling which I had been told was legal. I now suggested to our friend behind the desk that it would suit me better if I could be paid the money we were discussing at a later date in pounds sterling.

I could see at once that I had cracked it. There would be no problem at all, he assured me, as long as Mr Raj would let him have a credit note for every piece I had written. He went on to say that the money would be in my hands within a week. Mr Raj added a quiet cautionary note that it would be more like two months.

So after nearly eight hours it had been established that my first problem of how to get the money in rupees was insoluble. But an astonishing solution had been found. While it was illegal for me to withdraw my own money in rupees in order to spend them locally in Bombay, it was apparently the simplest thing in the world to pay me overseas in foreign currency. One of India's most desperate problems is a chronic shortage of foreign exchange and yet with wanton disregard they were throwing money away.

This is the story as it happened to me. There may be excellent reasons for all that is written in India's huge foreign exchange control regulations. Of course, it was irritating to waste a day and a half like this, but everyone I met in that time was anxious to do all that they could to help me cash my cheque. It was not their fault that it was impossible. It was the way of the bureaucrats and is a good illustration of what can happen in India.

Incidentally, at the time of writing more than nine months have elapsed and I still have not had the money. But I am assured that its arrival is imminent!

FROM BOTHAM
WITH LOVE

I have always been amused by the ease with which
we journalists are able to score runs and take
wickets from the safety of the press box. I still find
I can score runs all round the wicket from the other
side of the boundary. But once, in India in 1963/64, I
came within an hour or so of actually donning white
flannel trousers and going out and trying to put it into
practice in the middle as an England player.

I was twenty-four and on my first tour as a
journalist. It looked as if England would only have ten
fit players for the Second Test match in Bombay.
During the First Test in Madras a virulent tummy bug
had swept through the side and none of those affected
had recovered in time for Bombay.

It looked as 'if it was going to be a matter of
coercing a convenient Englishman to make up

numbers. At a press conference the day before the match started, the manager of the side, David Clark, revealed the sorry state of affairs and the necessity of having a willing helper to call upon. He went on to say that the last two members of the supporting cast to have played first-class cricket were himself and me. He had captained Kent but had retired early in the 1950s, while the memory of my extremely lucky Blue at Cambridge in 1959 was a little more recent and perhaps I was still young enough to be fit.

It was decided then and there that I was to be first reserve. Having announced this to the assembled company of scribes, he suggested firmly but politely that I should try going to bed before midnight. With insufferable arrogance and I hope a smile, I replied that I would certainly play if needed, but that if I scored fifty or upwards in either innings I was damned if I would stand down for the Third Test match in Calcutta. I suspect that David's reply was unprintable.

I went to bed early, but I don't think I slept very much for I was full of nerves and excitement as it dawned on me that what, in my pre-accident days, had been my life's ambition might even now be realised in the most unlikely way.

It did not happen though, and understandably, if a trifle unluckily. Mickey Stewart, the England vice-captain, had heard the desperate news on his radio in hospital on the morning of the match. He immediately jumped out of bed and got dressed. He poked a pretty pale face round the door of the England dressing room about an hour before the start and my dreams of sudden fame were shattered. I was a little unlucky because England lost the toss and fielded in great heat and humidity, and Stewart was back in his hospital bed with a raging temperature by lunchtime.

My most embarrassing moment occurred in the intransit lounge at Bermuda Airport in April 1980. England had had an extremely unsuccessful tour of the West Indies under the enigmatic captaincy of Ian Botham who had turned out not to be the captain the selectors had hoped for. And since taking on the job, his own game had deteriorated alarmingly.

After the First Test match in Port of Spain, I had written in strongly outspoken terms in the London *Sunday Express* about Botham 's lack of ability as a captain. Someone had sent him a copy of the piece and he had stuffed it in his blazer pocket. For the rest of the tour our relations were distant, to say the least.

The next time he wore his blazer was on the journey home from Jamaica. The aeroplane did not leave Kingston until forty-eight hours after the Fifth Test match had finished. Soon after getting on board Botham delved in his pockets and found the offending piece. Being on the tired and emotional side, not surprisingly, it upset him.

We landed in Bermuda for a refuelling stop. Blissfully unaware of all the chat my article had provoked half a dozen rows in front of me, I got out to stretch my legs. Not long after we had got into the intransit lounge I went to the loo. When I came out Botham was immediately outside the door and said something which I did not hear although I then heard Bernard Thomas, the team's physiotherapist, cautioning him.

In the main lounge Thomas then instigated an impromptu physical jerks session which he later told me he had done in order to keep Botham occupied. The exercises stopped a few minutes before the reboarding call. I was standing with some other journalists in a comer of the room. Suddenly I looked up and saw Botham approaching me, saying that he wanted a word with me. He suggested that I accompany him to another part of the lounge.

Realising exactly what was going to happen, I

declined the invitation reckoning that if I stood my ground with everyone around me, it might deter him from violence. I said that I thought the present geographical situation was as good as any other. Seeing the size of him I was dead scared. As I would not move he began to express himself in extremely forthright, if not entirely lucid, terms about the article I had written about his captaincy. Then he became more general but no more complimentary.

While he was talking he began to prod me forcibly in the chest with his right index finger. Gradually, the finger began to curl and I expected something more solid.

While the initial exchanges had been taking place, quite a gallery had gathered. Then, just as the situation became a trifle critical, Bernard Thomas and Dudley Doust (who was writing a book with Botham) appeared behind him and led him reluctantly away from me. But he soon broke free and charged back to me taking me by the shoulders and throwing me against the wall. I fell back into one of the chairs against the wall and stayed down while Bernard and Dudley recollected their charge. I went over to my colleagues and we all agreed how disgraceful it had been. I am sure I was still shaking when the time came to reboard the aircraft.

On the first leg of the flight I was in an aisle seat and the seat on my left, the middle seat, was empty. When I returned I found that it was now occupied by a blonde of ample proportions. I was sure after a quick glance that her boob measurements would have set some sort of a record.

No sooner had I sat down and fastened my seat belt

than I heard an angry noise in the gangway behind me and I saw Botham approaching with his arm raised. The storm signals went up. I took off my glasses and surreptitiously passed them under cover of my left arm in the direction of my new neighbour, for I did not want them broken.

My assailant arrived with a few more well-chosen epithets and stood over me. I continued to pass my

glasses sideways and encountered soft resistance. I continued to push and only fully appreciated the full extent of her chest measurements when she rocketed about eighteen inches into the air, expressing her displeasure as she went with a loud, 'Do you mind!' With enemies on both sides of me I was in a difficult situation. Mercifully a steward arrived and steered England's captain away from me and back to his seat. I then explained my actions to the irate blonde who was still not entirely convinced.

During the flight to London, masses of journalistic conferences took place. We all agreed not to write anything about the incident. We arrived at Heathrow on a Saturday morning. The following Sunday week I was at my house in Norfolk and before breakfast I was glancing through the newspaper headlines when I saw Botham's name in large letters on the front page of the *People*. There was also something about a fight with a journalist, so I grabbed the paper. To my horror I saw my own name in the second paragraph. The story had been well and truly leaked although it was never admitted. Probably one of the journalists on the aeroplane had spoken indiscreetly in a Fleet Street pub.

My telephone rang all day, and from as far away as Australia. The authorities at Lord's wanted to hear my version and so too did Alan Smith, the England manager on that tour, who had stayed on board during the Bermuda stopover, while newspapers and radio stations wanted quotes. Eventually, Ian Botham and I made it up and had a well-publicised drink in the pavilion at Southampton soon after the start of the season.

No one enjoys criticism and after a long and

disappointing tour, Botham's reactions were quite understandable. Whether they were justifiable as my great friend and *Guardian* colleague, Frank Keating, wrote in a book, I am not so sure.

A LOAD OF BULL

We have all heard of cricket matches being stopped by dogs running onto the field; cats have occasionally stopped play and so have over-curious seagulls and pigeons, although more rarely. I daresay that in the outback of Australia some more remote games of cricket may have been held up by kangaroos. But I had the luck, although it did not look like that at the time, to be present on what must surely be the only occasion a county match has been held up by a bull.

I was nine or ten in the late 1940s when Norfolk were busily engaged at Norwich in a Minor County match against Kent Second Eleven. I shall remember the names of the members of that Norfolk side long after more famous cricketing names have been forgotten. They were my first heroes and what giants they seemed to me.

The County's fortunes were, to say the least,

inconsistent. I watched every ball of every home match avidly, from a deckchair in front of the small wigwam-like tent which was taken every year by my father at Lakenham cricket ground. Wonderful to relate, Norfolk were having just about their best day ever in those immediate post-war years. Kent had made more than 300, but Norfolk were fighting in the most stirring manner. Brian Clements and Eric Edrich, who played for Lancashire before that and who was the brother of England's Bill Edrich, were hitting the ball all over the place.

Our tent was at square leg and I can still remember the excitement of fielding the ball as it raced over the boundary. It was heartbreaking when Clements just missed his hundred, but I could hardly contain myself as Norfolk approached the treasure trove of a first innings lead. A mere handful of runs were needed and I was perched tautly on the very edge of my deck chair when suddenly a commotion began in front of the huge (for a ten-year-old) thatched pavilion. Play was held up and I watched in miserable frustration as a gigantic bull trotted down the pavilion steps. With a resounding snort and a wave of its tail, it cantered belligerently out towards the pitch.

It took a moment or two to sink in and then the players fled in what I considered to be the most disgusting exhibition of cowardice. Of course I was sure the visitors who were in the field were to blame. Most of them raced to the sightscreen and hid ignominiously behind it while the bull snorted afresh and galloped furiously round the square. By now the crowd had begun to take evasive action as the bull, having been cheated of the players, turned its attention to the rows of benches behind the boundary on the far side of the ground. To my horror, my family and all those around my deckchair roared with laughter. I remained deeply upset by the entire performance. Would the batsmen 's concentration be upset and what about that first innings lead?

We discovered later that the bull had escaped from the Norwich cattle market and had set off at great speed, leaving its pursuing handlers far behind. It was obviously a bull with a keen sense of direction, for to reach the cricket ground from the market place required a sound knowledge of the side streets. It was clearly a bull of considerable intellect. Now, as it turned on the crowd, the handlers arrived somewhat breathlessly in front of the pavilion. To my immense relief they soon trapped the bull in a far comer of the ground.

But not for long. The animal shook itself free and set off at an even greater pace than before, bang across

the middle of the ground to some neighbouring allotments. Without a moment's hesitation it dived through the fence and into the assorted vegetables, mercifully never to reappear. Fifteen precious minutes had been lost and to my horror I found that it was generally thought to have been hysterically funny.

Can you imagine? The game had been- held up at a thrilling stage, the pitch might have been damaged and the batsmen's concentration irrevocably upset. As it turned out, by the end of the day my happiness was complete, for Norfolk passed 400, Edrich reached 170 not out and I was able to forget all about that wretched bull although I had to talk severely to my parents about all that laughter.

Probably the most amusing press box story at which I was a spectator involved two famous old Australian cricketers, Jack Fingleton and Bill O'Reilly. Australia played the Fourth Test match against the West Indies at the Adelaide Oval at the end of January 1969. In the final innings Australia made a wonderful start when chasing a target getting on for 500.

The West Indians were beginning to panic and Charlie Griffith was bowling to Ian Chappell with Ian Redpath at the non-striker's end. The Australians needed every run they could get and there had been some near suicidal short singles. Griffith ran into bowl and then stopped in his delivery stride and saw that Redpath was already three yards down the wicket, backing up.

The time-honoured procedure on these occasions is for the bowler to warn the batsman the first time and to run him out the second. But Griffith promptly took the bails off the first time, appealed and Redpath was quite correctly given out.

When this happens it always causes unpleasantness. In the next morning's papers Griffith was roundly condemned for his actions. Only two writers took Griffith's side and they were Bill O'Reilly and Keith Miller, neither of whom would have dreamed of trying to get a batsman out in this way.

In the press box the following morning Jack Fingleton took Bill O'Reilly to task, telling him that he would never have done the same thing himself in a million years. O'Reilly, who was sitting in the row in front of Fingleton, half turned round and said in a loud voice, 'When I was bowling I never met anyone that keen to get up the other end.'

Game, set and match to O'Reilly.

I was lucky enough to play in Keith Miller's last game of first-class cricket. In 1959 when I lurched into that Cambridge side, we played against Nottinghamshire at Trent Bridge. Nottinghamshire's captain, Reg Simpson, had persuaded Keith to turn out as a guest star.

There was a good crowd on the Saturday when I dropped Keith from a skier in front of the ladies' stand at deep mid wicket. Sitting in the ladies' stand that day was Beverley Fleitz who was a former Miss Australia. She went on to marry Jack Hilton. I was almost certainly concentrating more on her than the cricket.

Keith made 60 or 70 in the first innings and a hundred in the second and on the last day Cambridge were asked to make an impossibly huge score to win. I went in first and by a great piece of luck was still in at lunch. We had lost a wicket or two during the morning and although I had managed to stay there I only got about twenty in two hours as I scratched about. Whenever I hit the ball in the middle of the bat it went unerringly to a fielder.

At lunch I sat next to Keith and I complained bitterly about the way I was playing. Keith listened and then asked me if I thought I was better than the bowlers of whom he was one. I told him that of course I was not.

'Right, of course you're not,' he replied. 'And you've done well to stay there. If you'd been better than the bowlers you'd have had 70 on the board and you wouldn't be complaining.'

It was a marvellous piece of horse sense for anyone starting in any game.

007 GETS HIS MAN

The name Blofeld has always been difficult to get across to telephone operators and hotel receptionists. Es and Is and Ws creep in to unexpected places and the F often appears as an S. But there has usually been a gasp of familiarity from those acquainted with the Machiavellian dealings of one Ernst Stavro Blofeld who has occasionally been glimpsed on the cinema screen stroking a white cat.

When Ian Fleming wanted an evil name for the head of Spectre in *Thunderball*, he wandered one morning into Boodle's, his club in St James's Street in London and idly picked up a list of members. His eyes soon settled on three Blofelds, my father, my brother and myself, and he looked no further.

At the time, fiction had known no more sinister crook than Ernst Stavro. He kept coming back into our lives with his annual fights to the death with James Bond, although the ultimate fate was one they both miraculously managed to avoid. It was all right with me, if Ernst Stavro made life easier for hotel receptionists.

When I was in Jamaica in 1961 staying in Ocho Rios on the north coast, I went to dinner with Ian Fleming at Goldeneye, his house in the banana port of Oracabessa further along the same coast. It was a memorable evening, not least because one of my fellow guests was Noël Coward who had a house at Port Maria.

Coward was in tremendous form. He hardly drew breath all evening and was hysterically funny. In bidding an effusive farewell at the end of the party, he asked me if I would like to drive over and have dinner at his house one night. Of course, I could hardly believe my luck and he added that he would call me in the morning at the Jamaica Inn where I was staying.

It must have been about half past ten the next day when the telephone rang in my room. When I picked it up a voice which sounded all too familiar and yet which, with a slight hangover, I could not instantly place, asked to speak to me. I replied that it was indeed me who was talking. The voice said, 'This is Noël Coward. I don't know if you remember but we met at Ian Fleming's place last night for dinner.' Not bad, as throwaway lines go.

It was the Blofeld coincidence which enabled me to strike up one charming and, I suppose, unlikely friendship at the business end of a long taxi queue on a wet afternoon in London. About fifteen years ago, I arrived at Waterloo Station to find that it was raining in such torrents that even parts of the Underground were flooded and so I took up my position in a taxi queue which at first sight seemed to stretch for miles.

Eventually, after what had seemed about a day and a half, I found myself at the head of it. Soon an empty taxi arrived. In a sudden and unexpected burst of altruism, with the door half open, I turned to the others in the queue behind me and asked if anyone wanted to come to Chelsea. At once, my offer was accepted by a svelte, elegant and extremely attractive lady.

It had never happened to me before, for every time I get onto an aeroplane I am never the one to sit next to that fantastic blonde. In fact, I always seem to get either babies on a mission to scream or bouncing men who race through their first two divorces and are well into the current passion before we have even been told to fasten our seat belts.

We introduced each other and she told me her name was Lois Maxwell and that she lived near Sloane Avenue. The taxi squelched its way over Westminster Bridge and was halfway round Parliament Square when my companion asked me how I spelt my name. With great alacrity I gave her H-E-N-R-Y.

'No,' she came back, 'the other one.'

So, I tried again, B-L-O-F-E-L-D.

'What an extraordinary coincidence,' she said grinning. 'I've played Miss Moneypenny in all the James Bond films and I've just come up from Hastings where we've been filming *On Her Majesty 's Secret Service.*'

'So you might almost say that we have a common bond,' was, I am ashamed to say, my immediate reply.

A RUM PUNCH

I have been lucky enough to have been eight times to the Caribbean which is such a delightful and spontaneous part of the world, even if the pressures of racism have sadly caused a few recent problems. The islands are as different and fascinating as the people.

Without doubt, the most intriguing person I have met in the West Indies is Sir Lionel Luckhoo, who comes from Guyana which is perched almost at the top of the Atlantic side of the South American mainland. He is a barrister of considerable fame whose family are hardly less remarkable than Lionel himself. The family has its origins in Lucknow in India.

Lionel has found a place in the *Guinness Book of Records* as never in his legal career, which began before the war, has he had a client convicted of murder. At the moment of writing he has secured more than three hundred consecutive acquittals. Indeed, once or twice he has had to win an appeal and once even had to bring his case over the Atlantic to the House of Lords in London.

He is a man of many parts. For a time he acted for the notorious Jim Jones, the head of the strange religious sect who were allowed to make their headquarters at Jonestown in Guyana's interior. The life of the sect ended when almost all the members - men, women and children - committed suicide by drinking poison at Jones's instructions. Jones then killed himself. On one previous occasion on the telephone, Lionel had actually talked Jones out of committing suicide which he had promised to do when the authorities threatened to remove his adopted son from his care. Ironically, Lionel remembers this as the most significant failure of his life.

Lionel, who looks remarkably like Napoleon, found himself in London as Guyana's High Commissioner. Soon afterwards he was asked by the government of Barbados if he would act for them in a similar capacity. This double role produced many hilarious stories as he received a stream of double invitations. The only thing he refused to do was eat two dinners at the same party.

The story I like the most happened in Geneva at an important sugar conference. Both Guyana and Barbados were concerned that the chairman ship of a new body which was being set up should go to the same person. At the conference, Lionel was sitting in the seat reserved for Guyana. He rose to his feet and said that in the name of Guyana he wished to propose that such-and-such a person be elected as chairman. Then, he sat down for a moment before rising to his feet once again, saying this time that in the name of

Barbados he would now like to second the proposal that this same person should be elected chairman. This caused immediate consternation because never before had the same person proposed and seconded a motion and those in control were most unhappy. It did not seem right. Fortunately Lionel found the solution.

He asked if there was a place for the representative of Barbados. It happened that there was, over on the other side of the room. Lionel then got up and proposed the motion in the name of Guyana and sat down again before gathering his papers and himself together and walking across to the far side of the room to the seat reserved for the representative of Barbados. Whereupon, in the name of Barbados, he seconded the motion. This manoeuvre satisfied all the sticklers for the proper procedure.

Lionel has two brothers who, like him, are lawyers and Queen's Counsel and they also have both been knighted. Lionel who was twice knighted, tells a delightful story of how, after dubbing him on both shoulders with the sword, the Queen had said to him, 'You are looking very grave, Sir Lionel.'

'Yes, Ma'am,' he replied, 'I was considering what might have happened if you had taken the quickest route with the sword from my right shoulder to my left.'

'I can assure you, Sir Lionel,' the Queen answered with a smile, 'that it would not have been the first example of a headless knight.'

I drank the most absurd bottle of wine in my life sitting on the massive roots of a Stinking Toe Tree at Santa

Mission in Guyana. Following a two-hour trip by police motor launch up the Kimuné, a tributary of the Demerara River, we arrived at Santa Mission. Then after going round the indigenous Amerindian settlement we had our picnic lunch under the Stinking Toe Tree at the top of the rise above the landing stage.

I had met Diane McTurk at a dinner party in Georgetown and had mentioned that I was writing a book which was partly about the West Indies and partly about the England cricket tour. Diane's parents had been among the relatively early pioneers in the Rupununi in the interior. She suggested that I should visit Santa Mission which is the nearest Amerindian settlement to Georgetown and she promised to arrange it.

The police launch was waiting for us in the pouring rain after the twentyfive mile drive from Georgetown to Atkinson Field. We clambered aboard at a rickety old landing stage where incongruously there was a stall covered with Coca Cola advertisements. Then, we set off across the Demerara which was almost a mile wide and looked and felt twice as far. It is a huge river and by the time we reached the mouth of the Kimuné, we were soaked.

The Kimuné was small with very fast flowing steely black water. Our police navigators knew the channel intimately and steered us skilfully past any dangerous rocks, but they could not prevent the propellers becoming clogged up with the weed which grew in the water. Every so often we had to stop while one of them cleared the propellers. Each time the flow took us backwards at a terrifying rate.

Overhead the trees on each bank almost met,

enclosing us in a tunnel, for the tributary was not very wide. At times, there was nothing more than a slit of sky above and it was unnaturally dark, which gave it an eerie feeling. The trees, bamboo and the undergrowth were impressive, in a wild and primitive way. Diane told me that Amazon country was like this and of course the Amazon was not all that far south. We also saw some rather ugly looking magpie-like birds from time to time but not much other wildlife.

After about an hour's travelling through jungle we emerged into more open marshy country where at intervals the palms stood like sentinels as they presided over the scrubland below. Now there were more birds, but they were mostly black, ugly and disappointing. Before long, we came across a fishing boat with only children on board. Almost immediately after passing them our pilot pulled over to the left to a small landing stage.

There were more children and a couple of old men standing by who watched us very carefully as we landed. Diane started to talk to them and soon they began to smile and generally seemed to be on our side. The Mission was peopled only by women, children and old men. Diane explained that this was because the grown-up male population were away in the interior, working on the timber grants. They could be away for as much as six or even nine months at a time.

A boy in his early teens greeted us almost formally. He was apparently the headman's son. His father was away with the others and he had a certain seniority. He took us up the hill past the enormous Stinking Toe Tree and stayed with us while we were taken round the Mission. The community lived off the land and had no use for money.

We were taken into their neat houses, made from wooden poles, and watched the process of daily life. We saw how they built their houses, how they made the roofs, how they cooked their food and how they brewed their alcohol. We watched while the women wove stool seats and chairs from dyed palm fronds. We were in another world from cricket and the West Indies.

There was a fascinating story about the palm fronds they use for roofing the houses. If the fronds are not cut at the time of night when the moon has gone and it is still pitch dark - what they call in 'the dark of the moon'-a maggot matures inside the frond on the roof of the house and gradually eats the roof away until it eventually collapses. I was also shown trees which had a dry bean-like pod which rustled noisily in the wind and were known as the Chattering Women trees.

After our conducted tour it was lunchtime. The headman 's son had organised some other boys to bring our picnic basket and cold box up from the boat and we sat down on the roots of the Stinking Toe Tree. In the cold box was a bottle of Mateus Rosé which Diane had brought and which we proceeded to drink, watched by a considerable and embarrassing number of the children and old men. It was a bottle of wine that I shall never forget. After lunch the headman's son took the leftovers as his right and organised a washing-up party. Then, it was back to the launch and eventually to Atkinson Field and Georgetown before sun set after an extraordinary day in South America.

The Stinking Toe Tree was, as far as I can remember, given its name because some part of it gives off a disgusting smell when it rains.

After covering the 1980/81 season in Australia, I left Melbourne Airport one evening, spent the next night in London and had dinner the following evening in Port of Spain, Trinidad, where the next day England were to start a Test series. Being a glutton for punishment, I agreed to go that night to a calypso tent on Frederick Street where the principal performer was the Mighty Shadow, one of the top three or four calypsonians.

During the carnival season, each of the leading calypsonians has his own 'tent' which is a large hall somewhere in the city. These 'First Division' calypsonians are supported by their own entourage of singers who give themselves the most unlikely names. Each night they sing the calypsos they have written for that year's Carnival. The tents have a fantastic atmosphere of excitement, humour (even if most of it is pretty basic), and a strong sense of total involvement. The tents are just about full every night and this particular evening was yet another of pure uninhibited West Indian rhythm and enthusiasm.

As we came out at about midnight, the chatter and the grinning faces all round us told the story of an evening of uncomplicated and glorious fun. At this time of the year -January and February - Cricket, Carnival and Calypso are the three Cs in the West Indies and once experienced the atmosphere will never be forgotten.

That evening, three of us went along to hear the Mighty Shadow and his troops. There was Patrick Eagar, the famous cricket photographer, Jane Morgan, a BBC radio producer, and myself. When, at the end, we emerged into Frederick Street there were millions of people but no taxis. I was staying at the Queen's Park Hotel on the Savannah which was less than half a mile away and I suggested that we walk there and they could then get a taxi and go their respective ways.

Jane immediately asked me if it was safe to walk. I was very much caught up in the mood of the evening and assured her that it was just about the safest journey she had ever undertaken. So we set off.

After a shortish distance, an open piece of wasteland led off to the left. We were just about level with it when I suddenly heard a scuffle of gym-shoed feet behind and at the side of us. I half turned and three or four young men ran silently past us. As soon as they were past, the biggest turned round, half crouched and stood menacingly in front of us, his henchmen beside him. For a split second I thought of saying, 'My dear old thing, what on earth do you think you are doing?' But then I suddenly spotted a gleaming metal object in the right hand of the biggest of them and further inspection showed that it looked uncannily like a gun. Now, I have never had a gun pointed at me in this way before. The cops in New York were different, for I had felt then that they probably knew what they were doing. Now, I was not half so confident.

The gun was pointing unerringly at my tummy button, and then I saw that one of the others also had one which was wobbling slightly in the general direction of my navel. The next day I was asked if they were real guns to which I replied that I was in no mood to find out and was happy to go quietly. Actually, for a few moments, everyone just stood there and gawked. Then, suddenly I realised that it was a good old mugging. Wasting no time at all, I proceeded to win the gold medal for cowardice yet again. False heroics were out. With almost fevered speed I began to distribute all the worldly goods I could possibly find in my pockets which amounted to a hundred or two Trinidad dollars (about £30). I only wished there had been more in case they felt I was not trying. But as it happened they were so impressed with my eagerness to help that they forgot about my watch and signet ring.

Patrick went quietly too, although he had quite a lot more money on him, but poor Jane had a rough time of it. She had her passport in her bag and when they

had removed the bag she asked if she might have her passport back. For some reason they did not consider that to be form at all and promptly smashed her in the face. At that moment I remember wondering what James Bond would have done, but mercifully before I could come up with the answer they had fled.

Only minutes after they had run off across the wasteland, the police, who had been alerted by someone who had been watching, arrived upon the scene. With the help of their torches we looked over the ground in the direction in which they had run off and to our great delight we found Jane's passport and one or two other important items which they had emptied out of her bag. The police told us that, with all the overseas visitors, Carnival time was the mugging season in Port of Spain. A number of young Venezuelans came over each year especially for it. We were then taken back to the police station below the Hilton to make our statements.

After that, the other two were allowed home while I was plonked in the back of a squad car and driven round the streets of Port of Spain for a couple of hours looking for suspicious characters. I told the chap in charge that in my many visits to Port of Spain I had never seen anyone on the streets at two o'clock in the morning who did not look suspicious. Rather pointedly, he asked me what I meant and so I thought it was better to change the subject. Of course, we found no one and eventually I was dumped at the Queen's Park Hotel after another day which had in its way been both full and memorable.

AIR WAVES

My Test match broadcasting career only began because of an outrageous piece of deceit. In January 1972 I arrived in Kingston, Jamaica, at the start of New Zealand 's first ever tour of the West Indies.

I soon met Alan Richards of the old NZBC who was going to report the series back home, as well as doing commentary locally for the Caribbean Broadcasting Union. As part of a reciprocal arrangement, visiting commentators also work for the local network. The CBU had made the arrangements with NZBC before Alan left New Zealand. Not long after he had arrived in Jamaica, Alan was asked by someone he did not know if he was prepared to join their commentary team; he imagined it was the same lot and agreed.

Shortly after this he made the alarming discovery that in all the cricketing West Indian territories there are two radio stations. One is CBU while the other is part of the Rediffusion Group. Alan found, therefore, that he had accepted invitations to commentate for both stations simultaneously for the Jamaican leg of the tour.

When we met later that day he asked me if I had ever done any cricket commentaries. Sensing an opportunity, I immediately replied that I had and at some length I told him about my achievements, all of which, I need hardly add, were completely fictitious for I had never done a single word of live commentary. This did not worry me for I had listened avidly to cricket commentary since I was seven or eight and I supposed I should have had some idea of how to do it. Anyway, I was happily confident. It helped too that about five years before I had done a test commentary for the BBC to see if I was any good.

I remember being scared out of my mind as I did two twenty minute tapes at a county match and then, almost as frightened, I went to Broadcasting House and had to listen while they were played through by the Head of Outside Broadcasts. I still loathe listening to myself for I always think it sounds dreadful and I can never understand why anyone asks me to go on doing it.

Eventually, I got a letter from the BBC saying that it had been fine and that they had added my name to their list of commentators. Great excitement, of course, but five years later no other letters had turned up asking me to do any commentary. But at least it gave me some confidence in the situation I was now in.

The next day two guys from Radio Jamaica came to

see me and I continued the bullshit with renewed vigour. They bought it and by the time they left I had been asked to join Radio Jamaica's commentary team for the three matches on the Jamaican leg of the tour.

The other two commentators were both former West Indian players, Peter Bailey and Jackie Hendrick. Over the next three years I was to do a good deal of work with them and we always had tremendous fun. Deceitful though I had been, it all seemed to go pretty well. By the time the New Zealanders left Jamaica I had been asked to commentate by the sister stations in the other territories except Barbados, who got their knickers into a twist about a work permit.

The following two winters I was back in the West Indies, first with the Australians and then the Englishmen, and so by the time I came to do a Test match in 1974 for the BBC, I had well and truly cut my teeth in the West Indies and perhaps got my worst howlers out of my system. I had been very lucky.

For all that, I was still pretty nervous when I climbed up to the commentary box in Manchester in 1974. England were playing India and the match was badly affected by rain. But I remember it most, not for the cricket, but for one hysterical moment when, convulsed with laughter, I had to try and commentate. It has happened many times since. The atmosphere in the BBC commentary box is often very light hearted and a great deal of sniggering goes on. Of course, with open microphones, we cannot laugh out loud. It's rather like being in church when, just because one must not laugh, the most trivial things seem extraordinarily funny.

Almost all the humour in the box comes directly or indirectly from Brian Johnston, a supremely funny man. Even when he is not in the box, the rest of us continue to try and gag in the same way.

In the middle of this Test match, BJ was talking away while Tony Greig was bowling. 'And Tony Greig comes in again and bowls. So-and-so plays forward and again the ball goes down to Hendrick at mid on. Hendrick throws Greig an underarm catch and he now polishes the ball on his right thigh as he walks back to his mark. Greig now turns again, strides up to the wicket, bowls and So-and-so plays forward again and the ball rolls once more down to Hendrick who throws it back to Greig. And now, just to vary things a little, as he walks back Greig polishes his left ball.'

Instantly the entire commentary box began to shake with laughter. BJ's twenty-minute spell was up and although he was almost choking with laughter, he managed to hand over to me. As I got into his chair I was not only bursting with laughter myself, but also all I could hear around me were splutters of badly suppressed laughter.

I had to get on with it and putting my hands up on each side of my face like blinkers so I could not actually see the faces of those shaking with laughter - catching someone's eye would have been fatal - I just managed to stumble on. I, and I suppose the whole of my broadcasting career, was perilously close to collapse in those few seconds.

Sharing a box with BJ is a bit like walking through a minefield. He constantly reduces everyone to hysterics, and is also a great practical joker. In England, listeners send us all sorts of booze and food, especially cakes. When the Australians are in England BJ usually waits until Alan McGilvray has his mouth full of the most delicious chocolate cake and then asks him a question. Multiple spluttering ensues.

He has an unnerving trick he plays on new commentators too. In England when it is raining and there is no play we go prattling on about everything and nothing, sometimes for two hours on end. It often gets splendidly out of control.

I usually leave the box when I have finished a spell of commentary to have a breather. I went out at one stage while it was raining in this Test against India and about half an hour later I climbed back to the box. As I came through the door I heard BJ, who was sitting in front of a microphone, say, 'And what better person to

take you through the full career details of the Indians, both the batting and the bowling figures than Henry Blofeld who has just come into the box.'

He immediately got out of the commentator's chair and everyone else looked at me as I took his place. The only person who might have been able to help me, Bill Frindall our scorer, had gone and it was panic time. Frantically I looked around, with words stammering out of my mouth, and I was met with impassive stares from the others.

With my heart beating at about a hundred miles an hour, I started to explain, very hesitantly and nervously, why I had not got the full career details of the Indian players at my fingertips. I was in the process of making a complete fool of myself when howls of laughter from behind made me realise that the microphone was dead after all and that we had handed back to the studio. It took years off my life. In the same match the Maharajah of Baroda, who was helping us out, was caught the same way.

One of the most dramatic pieces of commentary I have done was in Lahore in Pakistan when a Test match was held up by a riot. For about half an hour I kept it going live back to England. It all began when Mudassar Nazar was 98 and played a ball to long leg for a single. Many of the crowd thought it would go for two and ran onto the ground to congratulate Mudassar who was still on 99.

The civil police in their khaki shorts and lathi sticks came on to remove the spectators. One of them unwisely chased a small boy and when he caught him proceeded to belt him with his stick. The public do not much care for the civil police and they came over the boundary fence in their thousands and chased them off the ground.

The rather more formidable military police then arrived, which put a different complexion on things. With the help of canisters of teargas they cleared the ground. When Mudassar reached three figures soon after the game restarted I was able truthfully to say that he had reached a 'riotous hundred'. The next day it was even worse when a political riot began between the supporters of ex-president Bhutto on one side and his opponents on the other. I think we were much nearer to open warfare that time, but sadly we were not on the air.

The most idiosyncratic commentator I have ever worked with was Raffie Knowles in Trinidad. Alas, Raffie is now dead, but no more enthusiastic lover of sport, commentator and lover of people ever existed. When he was young he played most games at a fair level and represented Trinidad at hockey. He was a legend in Trinidad and was universally loved. His cricket commentaries were individual, even if they communicated the excitement rather than an exact description of what actually went on. 'And Vanny Holder bowls to Stackpole and Fredericks is jumping around there' was what Raffie considered to be an adequate description of Stackpole being caught at forward short leg.

Raffie was passionate about horses too. When commentating on a race down in the oilfields at Point-a-Pierre in which one of his own horses was running in a biggish field, the excitement and the decibel level broke new records in what appeared to be a one horse race. It subsequently transpired that Raffie's horse had finished seventh.

In the West Indies spectators bring their transistors to the cricket and often when broadcasting there is a huge volume of feedback which distorts the broadcast. Raffle's hold over the public was never better illustrated than that at those moments when he would say over the air, 'Come on fellahs, turn those transistors down, give us a break.' And within moments not a single radio could be heard. In the other islands the result of this appeal usually is that they are turned even louder.

What an experience it has been to share commentary boxes with such greats as John Arlott, Alan McGilvray, Brian Johnston and Tony Cosier and to have heard Jim Swanton and Jack Fingleton summarise play. Really, it has been a guinea a minute, with the laughter and humour which goes with it all.

In the commentary box, especially before John Arlott retired, cricket and wine have been two close companions. There was the splendid occasion during a Lord's Test match when we said over the air that we had run out of champagne and within an hour and a half a delivery van had arrived from Fortnum and Mason in Piccadilly with a case. It was a present from a listener.

UP FROM THE CELLAR

Considering the title, perhaps there has not been quite enough booze in this book. It goes without saying that along the way a multitude of bottles of all shapes and sizes, and often with extraordinary origins, have unleashed a remarkable waterfall of the most delicious wines, some of which have led to my periodic downfalls which have been illustrated in the previous chapters.

For all that, one of the best days I can remember was a marvellous cricketing adventure and yet was exclusively about wine. Each year in England, Old Boy elevens from the main public schools contest *The Cricketer* Cup competition which is sponsored by Moët & Chandon who need no introduction even to irregular drinkers of French champagne.

The prize for the winners is a visit one Sunday in October to Epemay and La Maison Moët & Chandon. Ben and Belinda Brocklehurst, who own *The Cricketer*

International magazine, nobly asked me to accompany the winners in 1982 and you may be sure that I made the most of it.

The day had an almost discouragingly early start and we all had to gather at Gatwick Airport at about eight o'clock in the morning. The old boys of Winchester had won the competition and they and their wives and girl friends and the London based representatives of Moët filled the aeroplane. The flight was given a marvellous start for no sooner were we off the ground than the first corks were popped.

It was a wonderful day, not only for the superb lunch at the Château de Sarran, the Moët headquarters, and for the formidable wine, but also for the hospitality and friendship of those who showed us round. We went round Hautvilliers which was the Abbey where Dom Perignon made his first champagne; we visited the cellars in Epemay which stretched for no less than eighteen miles and where they apologised in almost abject fashion for being almost out of stock as they only had about 190 million bottles. Mercifully, 1982 had been a brilliant year and they hoped it would be some time before the stocks were again so low.

I saw a champagne bottle, with cork and wire and tinfoil in position, opened with one stroke of a sword; it was most impressive. I drank some unforgettable Marc de Champagne, an enormous quantity of a number of different champagnes and I returned home with a new bottle of Marc as my own particular loot given to me by Henri Perrier, one of our guides. The following afternoon I caught a 747 from Heathrow to Sydney, and it did admirable duty as a hospital ship.

That visit to Epernay was one of the most

marvellous days I can remember, but it is still only just ahead of another wonderful 'wine' day which is the annual visit to 'Windy' Hill Smith's Yalumba Winery in the Barossa Valley. 'Windy's' hospitality is as impressive as Moët's. Wine flows like water and the only problem is to find someone who is sober enough to drive you back to Adelaide at the end of the day.

The visit to Yalumba always used to take place on the rest day of the Adelaide Test match but nowadays there are no longer rest days and as a result it cannot always be fitted in. Whenever it is, as many as 250-300 people take full advantage of 'Windy's' superb hospitality and often it is a day which produces dramas. The most significant was perhaps in 1975 when, in the middle of the series in which Dennis Lillee and Jeff Thomson destroyed England 's batting, Thomson almost destroyed his shoulder playing tennis at Yalumba. He took no further part in the series.

Nowadays, helicopters fly in the most celebrated of the players and radio microphones and television cameras are there to record it all. Each year the Hill Smith family come up smiling and lay it on better than ever before.

Ben and Belinda Brocklehurst were also responsible for arguably the most bizarre cricket tour I have ever been on. Besides running *The Cricketer*, they also own a holiday travel firm and each summer a few years ago took over a taverna in Corfu. Every two weeks a new group went out and those that travelled in late September and early October had to be able to make up a cricket side.

The Cricketer played three games against the local Greek teams on the Square in Corfu Town itself. There are in Corfu, two legacies of sixty years' rule by the English in the first half of the nineteenth century; cricket is one and ginger beer is the other.

In most unlikely parts of the world where cricket is played, the participants are usually expatriates from cricket playing countries, but not in Corfu. The Greeks play amongst themselves with a keenness at times bordering on a ferocity which would make Anglo-Australian Test matches seem small beer in comparison.

The rules are a trifle strange and the games are 33-over affairs. No one explained satisfactorily why it was 33 overs. It is played on a tarmac pitch covered by matting and part of the outfield on one side is the tarmac-ed coach park. If you are batting when there are no buses around, hitting a four is harder work than when the park is full. It is a four under a coach.

The setting is as beautiful as it is unlikely. There is a medieval castle at one end and a prim-looking Victorian bandstand at the other. Over the road behind the coach park is the sea and a restaurant that supplies superb calamari and retsina. Behind the other square boundary there are chairs and tables in amongst the acacia trees where the spectators, who participate in everything and sometimes give advice which would do credit to the Hill at Sydney, sit and drink their ouzo. And further back still is a row of shop fronts and houses which is a deliberate copy of the Rue de Rivoli in Paris. It is all wonderfully picturesque.

On the field it is very much a matter of Greek meets Greek. The elderly captain of Gymnastics who was called Contos, was undoubtedly a mean cricketer but not a bad performer with bat or ball. With the bat he was throughout a long and eventful career unable to countenance even the faintest possibility that he might ever be out.

On one memorable occasion he was comprehensively bowled, whereupon he walked menacingly down the pitch towards the umpire, bat upraised in a manner which would have had W. G. Grace's whole-hearted approval. As he came closer, the umpire shuffled uneasily and then, with a convulsive jerk, turned to the scorers with his arm outstretched and shouted 'No-ball'. Contos then returned purposefully to his crease, replaced the bails and prepared to face the next ball.

One of the richer characters I have met in my cricketing life I can only just remember for I was very young. In Norfolk, Audrey Buxton was universally known as Aunt Audrey and was a legend, albeit a terrifying one, for young children. She was obsessed with cricket and ran matches for children between the ages of about seven and ten. Aunt Audrey organised my first cricket match, just as she had organised the first cricket matches in which both my mother and father played as children.

She lived in a village called Bisley where she conducted these games on a neighbouring pasture which permanently housed a herd of cattle. She presided over events like the benevolent autocrat she was. If the game began at half past two, the cattle were probably not moved off the field until the fielding side went out. This meant that their most recent offerings were still hot and steaming when play began and formed an unnatural hazard.

The pitch itself was virtually indistinguishable from the rest of the field except for the faintly marked creases and of course the stumps. Aunt Audrey umpired at both ends and woe betide anyone who had the temerity to question a decision. Nonetheless, proceedings were conducted with an admirable fairness even if the decisions seldom bore any relation to the rules of the game.

For example, if you had to come more than fifteen miles to play – this was in the days of acute petrol rationing - it did not matter how many times you appeared to be out, Aunt Audrey insisted that you made twenty and saw to it that you did. On the other hand, if you were rather good and big-headed too,

Aunt Audrey, who was small and extremely frightening and who had a voice a Regimental Sergeant-major would have envied, would soon send you packing if you were a batsman or reduce your figures to ruin if you bowled.

If she felt that someone was out or felt that they had been in for long enough, she did not wait for anyone to appeal before sending them on their way. I sometimes have dreams about Aunt Audrey umpiring a Test match in which Dennis Lillee was playing. She would not have stood any nonsense with aluminium bats. Cricket today badly needs an Aunt Audrey or two.

I mentioned the Maharajah of Baroda earlier in the book and he, unwittingly, provided one of the funniest moments of my life. In October 1976, five of us, including Johnny Woodcock, the cricket correspondent of the London *Times*, drove from London to Bombay in a 1921 Rolls Royce and a new 1976 3.5 litre Rover. It took us forty-six days and nights and was an unbelievable experience. I hope one day soon it will be fully chronicled in a book of its own.

The last night but one before we got to Bombay, where Johnny and I had to be for the start of the England cricket tour of India, we stayed with the Maharajah at his Palace in Baroda. In fact, we were rather miffed because we were put up in the second palace which was just down the drive from the first. But as *quid pro quo* for this, Johnny and I had agreed to speak to the Baroda Cricket Association in the grand hall of the number one palace.

We all gathered on the balcony over the main entrance to have a drink before the start. When we eventually went downstairs, we were led into the big hall where about a thousand people gave us a hero's welcome. The Maharajah made a speech of welcome and then it was over to us.

We thought we had better pull out the stops so we both did about twenty minutes on our own at the end of which we were given another massive demonstration of support. Then, we went into a double routine and for about forty minutes we gave it to them straight from the shoulder before sitting down to the sort of reception reserved for Conservative Prime Ministers of England after addressing the Conservative Party Conference.

We felt rather pleased with ourselves and we returned in considerable good humour to the balcony. One of the Maharajah's retainers was the former Indian captain, Vijay Hazare. Johnny lent across and asked him how many of the thousand strong audience would have really understood all that he and I had talked about. Vijay paused for a moment and then shook his head from side to side, saying as he did so, 'Practically no one.'

Then there was the time in April 1980 in Sydney when I went to the Royal Sydney Agricultural Show and watched the world champion axemen in action. I was allowed to walk out on the grass and I found the axemanship quite remarkable. There was one performer who stood on a fallen tree trunk and, cutting a cleft between his feet, chopped the trunk in half.

Each time the axe came down it missed the toe of his boot by millimetres. When it was all over I asked him if they ever cut their toes off. He told me that it sometimes happened. So I asked him why he did not wear metal toe caps on his boots. He looked at me in horror and said, 'What, and ruin a good axe?'

Then, there are the stories of all the Christmases I have spent abroad, headed by the occasion when I arrived at Melbourne Cathedral, late for the eight o'clock service, and pushed my way in through a creaking door. I found a moment or two later that I had come in at the wrong end and was in the middle of the bishop and all his assistant clergy - all this, only to see

Johnny Woodcock sitting about twenty rows back in a crowded cathedral laughing his eyes out.

There was the cat that died on Christmas Eve on my verandah at the Gymkhana Club in Lahore in 1978.

But that and many others will have to wait until another time, and by then there will, I am sure, be many others that have not yet happened.

HAVE YOU HEARD
THE ONE ABOUT...?

In a life of continual travel which is always bringing me into contact with entertaining extroverts, I frequently find myself listening to the 'latest funny story'. The one thing that most so-called funny stories have in common usually seems to be a terrifying unfunniness. I can think of hundreds of occasions when I have had to burst into guffaws of artificial laughter at the end of stories and once or twice I have been left very red faced when I have laughed at the wrong moment.

But every now and then I come across a marvellous story which I try desperately to memorise and then experiment with on my long-suffering friends. One of the best of these was told to me more than twenty-four years ago, during my ill-fated sojourn in a stiff colla and a bowler hat in that merchant bank in the City of London. This story has become my trademark for the simple reason probably that it goes on for so long that most people have forgotten the beginning before I get to the end. In print, it's obviously impossible to pick up the different voice inflections or the changes of pace in the speech. For all that, I shall have a go, and off my long run too.

In the 1950s Wilkinson Razor Blades came onto the market and they had an advertisement on commercial television .A guy appeared on the screen with about four days growth on his face, put a new Wilkinson blade in his razor, shaved himself thirty-three times and did everything else about forty-eight times and then, looking totally exhausted, he held up a damp, rusty, dilapidated razor blade while he cried into the camera as if his life depended on it, 'And I've still got five shaves left.'

This is a story about a splendidly smart, pukka, upperclass English couple who lived in a marvellous house in the most fashionable part of London just behind Belgrave Square. They knew everyone worth knowing, it was even rumoured that some of them were from the palace and life was a constant stream of parties and champagne and doing the right thing at the right time. *Noblesse oblige* and all that. (It's awfully important to know exactly who you are talking about.)

One weekend the two of them decided that life was becoming too unbearably exhausting and hectic and that the following Wednesday they would repel all boarders and crash. For the next three days invitations were turned down all over the place and all was set for an early night. But just after he got back from his office, the telephone rang. She picked it up and the conversation went something like this, with a female voice at the other end of the line speaking first.

'Darling, guess what? Ronnie and Edith have just come in unexpectedly from the States. We're taking them out to dinner and Edith's just told me they haven't seen you for longer than they can remember. You simply must come and join us.'

'Angie darling, how sweet of you. But Bill and I have put tonight aside for early beds. And you know what he is, I don't think he'll budge.'

'I know exactly what he's like darling, but we're only just up the road and I can hear Eddie pulling out the cork as I speak. Tell Bill that if he comes quickly he'll get a glass of Dom Perignon and we'll let you go after one.'

Of course, one glass became three - you know the feeling too! The journey from Belgravia to the

Mirabelle in Curzon Street took barely five minutes at that time of night and after a frightfully good dinner, that basement in Berkeley Square called Annabel's was but a stone's throw away. Once they had settled in there, they drank the obligatory champagne. At half past twelve they were about to leave but just as they were about to climb the steps leading into the square where nightingales were once purported to have sung, a couple of old friends came bustling down and back they went.

She did lights out that night, and just before she clicked the final switch by her bed, her watch said thirteen minutes past three. The next time she opened her eyes she had the most ghastly and horrendous pain in her forehead and sensibly she shut them again pretty rapidly. Instinctively, she kicked across the bed and found her husband had gone to the office. Gratefully, she sank back to sleep.

When she next woke the pain was, if anything, even worse and the time was 10:37. As we all do from time to time, she knew it was an Alka Seltzer job and she lay on her back trying to pluck up the courage to get up. After about ten minutes she gave a convulsive jerk and pillows flew in a north north-easterly direction, duvets to the south-south-west, and everything else somewhere in between.

As she stood up her eye balls seemed to bounce painfully back at her off the wall and the bright light was ghastly. She shut them again pretty rapidly and, as we have all done from time to time, proceeded to the bathroom by means of the dry breast stroke standing up.

Putting her arms out in front of her and keeping her

eyes tight shut, she lurched from the end of the bed, to the wardrobe, onto the door post, off the light switch, against the passage wall, onto a cupboard and so on to the bathroom. It took her time to distinguish the hot tap from the cold. Then, she picked up an empty tooth glass, but she was shaking like a seismograph and it took her almost five minutes to fill it up. I hope you are still with me; it's quite simple so far.

Then, she felt around by the basin and located some of those Alka Seltzer that come two-by-two in tinfoil. After a considerable struggle she got both of them in the glass and, using the handle of her tooth brush, she fizzed them up and then, still with her eyes tight shut, she drained the glass. It gets more horrifying now.

Suddenly, at the back of her throat she felt the most ghastly, agonising and searing pain and when she opened her eyes wide for the first time that morning, she saw from the empty packet that she had managed to get one of her husband's brand new Wilkinson razor blades into the glass. Instinctively, she staggered back to her bedroom with the blood welling up against her taste buds as she went and she realised she ought to ring her doctor.

But when she got back to her bedroom she sat on her bed and then lay back. Nature, as it often can be on these occasions, was merciful and she went to sleep. When she woke again it was 3:37 in the afternoon and at once she tried a tentative swallow. It was sheer hell and again she started to think about her doctor. But then she remembered the long tradition of fortitude and bravery in her family. Her father had won an MC and Bar, her uncle something else and Bar and there was even a VC somewhere in the family. She knew her duty was to grin and bear it for as long as she could.

She was awfully brave too, and for a week she couldn't swallow and once she had swallowed she couldn't sick it up again. Then, one morning when she woke up she couldn't stop herself trying to swallow, and, would you believe it, the pain had gone. She leapt out of bed and for the next few days was full of the joys of spring as she played tennis, did vigorous press-ups and all the other physical exercises she enjoyed. After about five days of this she got out of bed and stretched and there it was again -the most agonising, biting pain at the bottom of her tummy on the right hand side. (It gets worse and worse, and more and more exciting.)

It bent her double and for the next week she could not sit down and once she had sat down, she could not get up again. It was unbelievably ghastly. But a few days later she staggered out of bed, stretched and, lo and behold, it had gone. It was back to the tennis courts and the press-ups with renewed vigour and enthusiasm. But four mornings later she stretched and - ooops - there it was again, an excruciating agony in the pole position on the grid, absolutely slap bang between her legs.

Now, she couldn't cross her legs and once she had crossed them, she couldn't uncross them again. And incidentally being a great enthusiast, she found it cramped her style no end. After two weeks she could stand it no longer and so she called her doctor, made an appointment and went round to his insulting room at 3:30 that afternoon. Sitting in eyeball to eyeball confrontation across his huge mahogany desk, she told him the entire story and when she had finished she said -wait for it -'Now Richard, I probably need some eye drops or some throat lozenges, but I need them quickly because it's awfully sore.'

'Yes, of course,' he said, 'but I never prescribe until I have had a look.'

She got undressed. He had a look. She got dressed again, sat down and continued the eyeball to eyeball confrontation across his desk. Coming from a cricketing family, she lent forward and asked him what the score was. The next bit goes very fast.

'It's not so much the score as the scorecard.' 'What do you mean?'

'Well, it's rather long.'

'Do you think I should hear it?'

'When's your next appointment?'

'In thirty-five minutes time.'

'If you promise to stop talking, I can just about get through it.'

'Then fire away.'

'Well, the day you did it you quite clearly gave yourself a tonsillectomy and the week after that you had an appendectomy and a week after that, I'm sorry to tell you, you had a hysterectomy. But that isn't the end of it by a very long chalk, I can assure you. Shortly after that you circumcised your husband and two days later you castrated a lover. And that's not the end of it either for very, very swiftly after that you removed the first two fingers of the right hand of a casual acquaintance. And then, and then,' (as he hesitated his voice rose) 'and then, and then you gave the vicar a harelip and what is more you've still got five shaves left.'

Phew! Don't try telling that one until you are word perfect and can rattle it off at great speed.Otherwise the audience will go to sleep or, worse still, start talking.

A good one I heard the other day is about the assistant in the vegetable section of a big supermarket.

He spotted an elegant lady over by the Brussels sprouts and went up to her.

'Good morning madam. Can I help you ?'

'Yes please, I want some broccoli.'

'I'm extremely sorry madam, but we don't have any broccoli. We've sold out. But madam, please don't despair, we have everything else you could wish for. We have Brussels sprouts, we have runner beans, we have broad beans, we have cabbages, cauliflowers, peas, turnips, vegetable marrows, spinach, courgettes, mushrooms -anything you might want.'

The lady clearly didn't want anything else for she walked away while he was still in mid-sentence. An hour later the assistant looked up again and, lo and behold, he saw this same lady standing in front of the vegetable marrows. He went over to her.

'Can I help you, madam?'

'Yes please. I want some broccoli.'

'Madam, how can I make it clear to you that we do not have any broccoli left. We have every other sort of vegetable there is. I am sure we can find a substitute for you.'

Once again, she walked away in silence. You can imagine the assistant's surprise when an hour later he saw her standing a few degrees south of the new potatoes.

'Can I help you, madam?'

'Yes please. I want some broccoli.'

'Madam, I have already twice tried to tell you that we don't have any broccoli. Let me try and explain it again. Madam, can you spell?'

'What do you mean, can I spell?'

'Well, madam, can you spell for me the dog in dogmatic?'

'The dog in dogmatic?'

'Yes, madam, the first three letters.'

'Of course I can. DOG,' she said, rather hesitantly.

'Very good, madam. Now try and spell for me the cat in catastrophic.' 'CAT.' She was growing in confidence.

'Brilliant, madam. And now my last question. Can you spell the fuck in broccoli?'

She looked horrified, appalled, and shocked and began eventually to stammer, 'But, but, but, there is no fuck in broccoli.'

'Precisely, madam. That is what I have spent mot of the last three hours trying to tell you.'

The other morning in London the telephone went in my flat. It was a great friend of mine who had just emigrated to Australia. He had arrived in Sydney the week before. I asked him how he was getting on.

He told me that the containers with his furniture had got there and that he was having a great time. But he told me that he had had an anxious moment at Sydney Airport. He had landed there at 6:30 in the morning and joined a long queue for immigration. When he eventually got to the front he handed his passport to a middle-aged Aussie with a huge beer gut.

He licked his thumb and worked his way through the passport. After repeating the process, he banged something into the computer and carefully examined the answer.

Then, he thumbed through the passport again, put something else into the computer, looked at the answer before turning to my friend and saying in the broadest of Australian accents, 'Mate, have you got a criminal record?'

My friend was understandably nervous at this turn of events and rubbed his hands a good deal while stammering out his reply.

'No, no, no, no, I'm frightfully sorry. I didn't realise it was still compulsory.'

I wonder how many Australian friends I've got left now.

And finally I must tell you about my visit to Leeds last year for the Test match. The wife of a good friend of mine had just had a baby and I went round to the local maternity hospital to visit her. I was shown into the waiting room and there were several other men there, presumably expectant fathers all trying to look calm and unflustered. After a few minutes the door opened and a nurse or a sister, wearing a starched hat which looked like the Eiffel Tower, came through the door with a broad grin on her face.

'Mr Thompson,' she said.

She looked around and a fairly rough chap in a T-shirt and jeans at the far end of the room got to his feet.

'Ay, I'm Mr Thompson,' in a broad Yorkshire accent.

The sister walked over to him with her right hand outstretched, saying as she went.

'Mr Thompson, I would like to be the first to congratulate you on becoming the proud father, not of one, not of two, nor of three, but of four fine bouncing boys. They are all doing wonderfully well, Mr Thompson, and your wife has come through her ordeal splendidly and is looking forward to seeing you. Mr Thompson, you must be over the moon to have four babies the first time off.'

'Oh, ay,' came the answer. 'But I'll tell you what, I expected more than one the first time.'

'You expected more than one the first time, Mr Thompson? What do you mean?'

'I'll tell you what, Sister, in the mill uptown where I work, every evening before I go home, I strip off and have a shower. And my work mates gather round and liken the lower half of my anatomy to a mill chimney. Ay, to a mill chimney. That's why I expected more than one.'

'A mill chimney, Mr Thompson. Oh ay.'

'Oh ay: he said, 'a mill chimney.'

'Then, Mr Thompson, I hope you'll let me give you a piece of advice?' 'Oh ay, what's that, Sister?'

'They may liken the lower half of your anatomy to a mill chimney. But if I were you, Mr Thompson, I'd get the bugger swept, as these four are black.'

I am sure a lot of my friends will accuse me of stealing their stories. If so, I can only congratulate them for

aving told me such good ones and, anyway, I regard
good stories as a form of duty-free international
currency.

CHEQUE MATE!

No cricket writer who has flown around Australia as much as I have in the last few years in pursuit of runs and wickets could possibly be immune to Dennis Keith Lillee. I am second to none in my admiration of Dennis as a bowler and I have seen him take a great many of his record number of test wickets. At times though, his behaviour has got right up my gullet. I have suffered Lillee throwing aluminium bats in Perth, kicking Javed Miandad also in Perth, and I have seen him bring a new perspective to the word 'sledging', which simply means abusing a batsman rotten. Of course, I have had a go at him in print, particularly in the columns of the Australian, which has several times put us on a collision course. Snarling and growling, he has passed me by on several occasions, but as I say, he bowls like an angel.

It was mildly ironic, to say the least, that soon afte

my last and perhaps most severe disagreement with Dennis that I should have found myself on the same platform in Adelaide, speaking on his behalf, at one of his benefit dinners during the 1981/82 season.

Midway through the 1981 tour of England by Australia, Lillee stayed in London while the team was playing, I think, in Northampton. Allan Border was also in London at the time. They were both involved in an incident at Lord's, with Jack Bailey, the Secretary of the MCC, when they attempted net practice during the Eton vs Harrow match, after having been told there would be no practice nets available that day.

I checked the story with Jack Bailey and wrote a strong piece about Lillee's behaviour in the Australian, which Lillee would not have enjoyed, although having behaved like that, I cannot see what else he can have expected.

Not long after this incident I had a telephone call from 5AD, the commercial radio station in Adelaide for whom I was covering the tour. They have a famous breakfast time double act of Bazza and Pilko and one of them asked me if I would speak one evening while I was in Adelaide during their next cricket season.

I said that of course I would and a week or two later I was told on one of my calls to 5AD that one of the other speakers would be Dennis Lillee and did I mind too much. I said that I didn't but made a strong condition either then or sometime soon afterwards that I would only do it as long as I was allowed to speak after Lillee. I felt that this way I would have some control over the evening if it became a slanging match.

Shortly before I arrived in Adelaide I discovered that it was a dinner benefit for Lillee at the East Torrens

Club. I hardly felt that I was the right chap to be performing on such an evening, but it was too late to pull out. I must say I did not look forward to it with any enthusiasm.

The evening arrived and it was with considerable fear and trepidation that I walked into the club. I was horrified to find that in the main hall, there was on one side the Henry Blofly Stand and in the other comer the Dennis Lillee Stand. I daresay it had been billed as the fight of the century. I was then taken downstairs to a sort of committee room where I was given a drink and told that I would be speaking before Lillee.

It was too late to do anything, but now I knew that I had been set up. A few minutes later the great man himself arrived to warm greetings from all and sundry. When it had died down a bit I tried, 'Evening Dennis, nice to see you.'

'So you're suddenly starting to be friendly,' came the unpromising reply. He went on to say in effect that the present situation did not change anything.

It was now that I understood fully Doctor Johnson's remark that if a man is to be hanged in a fortnight it concentrates the mind wonderfully, or words to that effect. In a mild panic, I went to have a pee and for some reason put my hand in my inside pocket and found my cheque book. Suddenly, the answer came to me. Standing where I was I pulled out my pen and wrote a cheque in favour of the Dennis Lillee benefit fund for one hundred dollars. I tore it out of my cheque book and left it loose in my pocket. Then, I returned to the fray feeling not necessarily that I had the joker up my sleeve but at least that I had a defensive weapon of a sort.

We soon went up to the hall and there were several hundred people there and their hero received a big cheer as he strode to his seat. I began to feel, not so much part of a contest, but like a tethered goat waiting for the tiger to pounce. After a couple of humorous speeches I was on my feet. After all this build up, what actually happened was a bit of an anticlimax really.

'I know I have had disagreements with Dennis Lillee,' I began to a good round of booing. When I said that we were all gathered here to pay tribute to a great fast bowler the applause was deafening. I then said that admiration for Dennis as a fast bowler was second to none, even if I couldn't always accept his behaviour. Silence.

'Just to prove that my heart is where my mouth is,' I went on, 'I would like Dennis to step up and accept this small contribution to his benefit fund,' and pulled out the cheque. I looked at Lillee who was sitting below the platform with his back towards me. He did not look round. 'If he won't come up to receive it, I shall have to go down and give it to him.' Of course this rather deflated the whole operation.

I left the rostrum, went down and stood behind Lillee and thrust the cheque forward. It still looked as if he did not want to acknowledge my presence, but I put the cheque in his hand and shook it at the same time and then scarpered back to the platform to await developments. I struggled through an assortment of stories which I did not tell very well and sat down to a modest round of applause, glad that it was over, but still apprehensive of the immediate future.

In time, Lillee himself got to the microphone and was reasonably mild in his criticisms of me. He said that journalists had their job to do, but he felt that personal criticism was going too far and that this was something of which I had been guilty. On the surface at any rate, we all finished the evening as friends. I must add that I was paid for my efforts and I felt that I had earned every single cent of it. When, two years later, I spoke at Rod Marsh's Testimonial Dinner in Perth, no one was quicker to offer his congratulations when I sat down than Dennis Lillee.

The evening ended with an assortment of Lillee's cast of cricket gear being auctioned and huge prices were paid for boots, trousers, cricket balls - especially the one he was using when he broke Lance Gibb's record and became the heaviest wicket taker in the history of Test cricket. One lovely lady even paid a small fortune for one of the great man's old jock straps and the benefit fund was suitably swelled. As a fast bowler who had taken more test wickets than anyone else, no one can have more richly deserved a bumper benefit.

FASTEN YOUR SEAT
BELTS FOR TAKE-OFF

Airports and aeroplanes inevitably play a big part in my life. I love flying, although like everyone else I am sure, I become acutely conscious of the fearful possibilities as we bump about with lightning flashing down the wings. When I first flew -in a lumbering old car ferry across the English Channel from Lydd to Le Touquet longer ago than I care to remember -I was petrified. It was many flights later before I became wholly unconcerned as I fastened my seat belt and waited for the first drink.

I well remember flying from London to Bombay in a Comet for the start of the England cricket tour of India in 1963/64. Even cruising smoothly along at 30,000 feet, it seemed to me to be the most horrendously dangerous pastime. Most crises in the air probably go no further than the flight deck, with the passengers gloriously unaware of impending doom. I always love being taken up to the flight deck too, for it seems to bring out the James Bond in me -all those switches and dials.

The first hairy moment I had in the air, well actually it was on the ground, was in 1961 on my honeymoon, flying from New York to Montego Bay via Nassau in a Boeing 707. We first had a technical hitch and a long delay in Nassau, and then when we eventually landed in Montego Bay (which then had a short runway), the aeroplane was uncomfortably reluctant to stop. We ended up a few feet from the end of the runway which was only a yard or two from the sea, where a year before a big aircraft had gone down with all hands.

We were met by a splendid Jamaican driver who was planning to take us to the Jamaica Inn in Ocho Rios, the most perfect honeymoon hotel in the world. A marvellous American couple had given us the principal suite for two weeks as a wedding present. It had been vacated by Richard Burton and Elizabeth Taylor just before we arrived.

When we had got into the car that night in Mo Bay, our driver with a fruity grin, pronounced on our landing in gravelly, Louis Armstrong tones, 'Man, Ah just prayed'. But his prayers were only partially answered for on the long drive to Ocho Rios his car suddenly ground to a halt with the big end irrevocably gone. It was pitch dark and it was hardly a promising position but luckily another taxi came past and we climbed in with some delightful Americans and found our way to Ocho Rios where a much appreciated bottle of champagne was waiting in an ice bucket in our suite. We drank half of it flat and tepid for breakfast the next morning when it was still pretty good.

I can remember being distinctly apprehensive about a prehistoric Dakota which I thought showed elephantine qualities, struggling down the runway in Calcutta on the way to Nagpur. On another occasion in India during a flight from Bombay to Ahmedabad, I was sitting next to Ken Barrington, formerly of the RAF, who suddenly noticed an unfriendly change in the engine noise although it brought no consequences with it. But that, mercifully, is, to date, the sum total of my nasty moments in the air.

Like most people who fly a lot, I have had my share of nasty and boring moments on the ground. I seem to

have spent almost half my life in crowded transit lounges at airports, waiting for reluctant aeroplanes to land or for the fog to lift or the baggage handlers to finish a union meeting or for a mechanical fault to be repaired. 'Mechanical fault' is a disquieting phrase which is used to cover a multitude of sins. You never quite know whether a wing is about to fall off or if it is simply a screw in a compass which has worked loose. Then of course, you and I always find ourselves sitting next to mothers with screaming babies and while we start the journey full of goodwill, we end it within a whisker of committing infanticide. My baggage is always the last case out of the aeroplane too.

I am one of those maddening people who likes to arrive at an airport in plenty of time and somehow I always end up by going to the airport with people of the get-on-when-it's-moving philosophy. I enjoy airports and VIP lounges and all that sort of thing. There are always things I want to buy and I look forward to that quiet drink before being herded into the wretched machine. But before that moment comes, I will have had to have done my packing, which is an operation I dread and loathe. But somehow I manage to get there with passport and tickets at the ready.

Or almost always, for I had a nasty shock at eight o'clock in the evening of Friday 14 October 1983 at the start of my journey to Australia for the Pakistan tour of 1983/84. I was clutching, among other things, most of the manuscript for this book. We had a bit of a champagne party at Anna's flat and, of course, she is the founding member of the get-on-when-it's-moving club. I did not have all that much time to spare when I clocked in at the appropriate check-in desk. My two bags had been ticketed and had gone through and I had got my boarding pass with the seat to be allocated at the gate.

'Can I see your passport?' asked the lovely girl who had checked me in. She wanted to make sure I had my Australian visa. It was 75 minutes to take-off.

I opened my zip handbag and to my horror and astonishment my passport was not there. Frantically, I searched my pockets but it was not there either. I had never done this before. Edward and Emma were standing behind the queue and when I broke the news, I suggested that Edward and I drove back like lightning to Anna's flat where it had to be. Anna, Suki (my splendidly mischievous daughter) and Angela had all gone to the loo.

Edward said he thought it would be better if Anna and he went for they might just possibly let me on without my passport. At the time this seemed good thinking, but of course airlines are heavily fined if they carry foreign nationals to Australia without the necessary visa. So there was no chance of that.

The other three now appeared, walking slowly back from the loo, laughing. I raced up in a panic and told them what had happened. Anna at once said that she knew I had the passport somewhere, but where? She and Edward decided to go back in his Daimler and no sooner had they gone than it suddenly occurred to me that the passport might be in the pocket of my suit carrier.

I rushed back to the desk where the girl was checking in another man and I saw that my suit holder was teetering on the edge of the moving luggage channel. I implored the girl to lift it back and she did.

I tore open the zip and there it was, my black passport. I snatched it out triumphantly, zipped up the bag, gave it back to the girl and told my girls to run and stop Edward and Anna.

They all went off in different directions while I waited behind the queue with my hand baggage. After about ten minutes the three of them reappeared but without Edward and Anna, for they had changed their minds and had gone in my car. We stood and looked at each other; there was nothing we could do and Angela made the most sensible suggestion which was that we should go upstairs and have a drink. I bought a bottle of champagne which we drank amid the stilted self-conscious conversation reserved for farewells. I hate goodbyes. My flight was now flashing on the Departures screen and so, although we had still not been able to get hold of Edward and Anna, I drained my glass, kissed everyone and fled.

I did not have time for any duty-free shopping and I set off on a long route march to Gate 29 and by the time I got there the first boarding call was being made. I was told that I would have to wait until the end before they could allocate me a seat. There were only about half a dozen people left when a voice behind me said quietly, 'Mr Blofeld'. I looked round and a chap from the desk came up to me and said most apologetically that as the business class was full they were giving me a seat in the first class section. Naturally, I was delighted and walked on board and was shown to seat lJ in the front row of the aeroplane.

I have never been looked after better, with excellent browsing and sluicing. We took six hours to reach Bahrein and after that it was seven to Singapore where

I decided to get off and buy some films. As passengers began to leave the aircraft an announcement over the Tannoy asked four people to report to the groundstaff. My name was the fourth to be called.

At the entrance I asked the steward what it was about and he did not know. In the passage a bespectacled Singaporean was pointed out to me. I told him who I was and he told me curtly that the aeroplane was overbooked out of Singapore, that first and business class were both full and that I would have to continue the journey in economy class. He was not even too sure that there would be a place for me there. I told him I was travelling on a fully paid business class ticket and I would not go further back than that. He said he would do what he could and added that I had been warned that this might happen before I had left London. This was untrue, and I told him so. Of course he did not believe me. I went ashore and as I was about to reboard a gent in a mustard yellow jacket waylaid me.

I had been travelling for about seventeen hours and I suppose it all got a bit out of proportion. I begged his pardon and said I would not travel except in business class. The yellow jacket scurried backwards and forwards in the aeroplane trying to force a lady to move back from business to economy. I was standing at the end of the tunnel leading up to the aeroplane and new passengers were pouring past me. Yellow jacket then said I would have to spend the night in Singapore and asked me for my baggage tags. I told him they were in the locker above my original seat and off he went again.

Then, I came to the conclusion that there was no

point in standing on what one mistakes for one's dignity in these situations. When he next appeared I told him I was after all prepared to slum it in the back.I had rather hoped that the news might please him, but if it did there was no outward sign. He then told me, rather surprisingly, for all passengers except me were on board, that he had not been able to find the lady he hoped to pitchfork back into economy. He bolted back into the aeroplane like a rabbit.

The groundstaff then began to close the entrance to the back of the machine and things were not looking at all promising when back he came beckoning me to join him. In the aeroplane my hand baggage was by the bulkhead and he gestured me to wait there while he buzzed off again. He returned, muttering something about it being all right and told me to follow him.

In the back of business, an attractive lady in bright blue was standing up and looking massively disgruntled. I could see from the way she looked at me that I was a very long way down her visiting list. When I drew level she told me that I had spent the first two legs of the flight in the front of the aeroplane and that she had already spent one leg in economy. I said as gently as I could that I had a fully paid business ticket. 'So have I,' she replied which shook me not a little. Yellow jacket had lost his voice so I then instructed him to lead me to my fate in the back. It was a smoker, and I couldn't see the film as the seat was by the bulkhead. As the yellow jacket left to go, I could not resist sending him on his way with a quick, 'I'll have your balls for this,' through clenched teeth.

My misery was complete when I had to wait an hour and a half after take-off for a drink. Two days after the event these escapades become extremely trivial and unimportant, but at the time they are infuriating and one becomes filled with pompous indignation. Four days after I got to Sydney I had even forgotten the name of the airline and if by any strange chance I should remember it, I have every intention of travelling with them again because really they do pretty well. But I must warn them, please do not do that again. I am being serious too, for ninety minutes without a drink is a long time.

Anyone who travels a lot has these hard luck stories to tell and when you sit back and think about them afterwards they are really quite funny. But I have never had the luck to find myself sitting next to a potential Miss World. Anyway I hope, dear readers, that none of you have the misfortune to find yourself sitting next to me.

After all that, it was marvellous to be back at the Sheraton-Wentworth Hotel in Sydney, beautifully run by those superb hoteliers, Peter Thompson and Leon Larkin. Here guests are presided over by the best concierge in the business, Tony Facciolo, but then he is worth a book on his own. I lay gratefully on the kingest sized double bed I had ever seen and started to fight a losing battle against jet-lag. Before I had left London, Suki had given me some smoked salmon and I had only eaten a small amount of it on the journey. So for three mornings in a row, I was up at four o'clock scoffing smoked salmon. I thoroughly recommend the timing for it has never tasted better.

Reading the papers over the next few days I could not help but wonder if I had ever been away from Australia. The boiling issue at the time was who was going to captain Australia. Some said Kim Hughes, some said Rod Marsh, no one knew for certain. Jeff Thomson had a writ out against the *Australian* and Phil Wilkins for an article he had written after Australia's World Cup disaster. By the way, the taxi driver who had taken me from Sydney Airport to the Sheraton was a keen cricket supporter and his family had come from Yorkshire.

'What have you blokes done to Geoff Boycott then?' was the first thing he said to me after we had left the airport. I almost asked him to turn round and take me back but I stuck it out and in the face of mounting hostility I enumerated Boycott's sins.

The Pakistanis arrived and a doctor immediately told Imran Khan that he should not play cricket for fifteen days. Zaheer Abbas, who had captained Pakistan on their recent tour of India, had not come with the main party because of 'domestic reasons'. It was more likely that these were simply umbrage that after being chosen to captain the side in Australia, the President of the Pakistan Board had overruled the selectors and appointed Imran. It was probably a Karachi versus Lahore issue. What's new, in fact?

But I really knew that I was back when, during the Pakistanis' opening match of the tour in Brisbane, the news came through that Dennis Lillee had been appointed as vice-captain to Kim Hughes in Western Australia. Lillee was currently not speaking to members of the Perth writing media, but deigned to give an interview to 6PR, a commercial radio station. He was asked if this meant that he had buried the hatchet with Hughes and that they were now friends.

'If I go into the bar and have a drink with a bloke, it doesn't show my sexual preference, does it?' Lillee replied with overwhelming tact, elegance and charity.

Yes, when I read that, I knew I was back in Aussie. But by then I had already eaten eight dozen Sydney oysters and ifl go on at this rate, they're in for a bad season too. Oh yes, and I almost forgot, Joh Bjelke-Petersen made it yet again in the Queensland election and gave a most marvellously uncompromising and militant interview afterwards.

By my reckoning, as I write this last paragraph, I

have got another 120-odd days to go. I wouldn't really have minded if I had come all the way economy class. It's great to be back.

ABOUT THE AUTHOR

C ricket has been at the centre of Henry Blofeld's life since he first leaned to play the game at the age of seven. His first cricketing mentor was Miss Paterson whose splendid swingers went both ways when she bowled to him at Sunningdale School. He somehow managed to pass an exam to get to Eton where he played cricket against Harrow at Lord's when he was fifteen. Until he was seventeen he played with some success as a wicket keeper and an opening batsmen, and was in the Eton eleven for three years from 1955 to 1957, the last year as captain. In 1956, at the age of sixteen, he score a hundred for the Public Schools against the Combined Services in their annual two-day game at Lord's, joining Peter May and Colin Cowdrey as the only other two schoolboy players to have done so.

Then in June the following year came a severe road accident when he gallantly took on a bus with his bicycle and took no further interest in this world for 28 days. He made a remarkable recovery, but never played cricket with such promise again. He went to King's College, Cambridge where he never scored a run against the examiners and was kicked out after two years. He somehow blagged his way into the Cambridge side in 1959 and had the luck to play in first-class matches against Denis Compton and the great Australian all-rounder, Keith Miller, making a first-class hundred against MCC at Lord's.

After a two-and-a-half year spell in the City of London, bowler hat and all, he decided to see if he could write about cricket. However, the first article he ever wrote was about a second eleven football match in 1956 for the *Eton College Chronicle*. It earned him a robust interview with the headmaster for being rude about Bradfield School which was not a particularly auspicious omen for a career in journalism.

The Times decided to use Blowers, as he is affectionately know, as a freelance cricket writer in 1962. The following year *The Guardian* decided that they would find a home for his cliches and he remained with them as a freelance until *The Independent* set up shop at the start of the eighties. By then the *Sunday Express* also provided a home. He also wrote for the *Observer* and the *Daily Telegraph*.

In 1975 he joined BBC's panel of cricket commentators when he joined the famous *Test Match Special* team for two one-day games against Australia. His years were spent watching county and a certain amount of Test cricket in England - there was only one year when he commentated on every Test for TMS - and in the winter he toured the cricket playing world. He probably watched more neutral series overseas than those involving England and he often worked for more than one newspaper and often the BBC as well.

For about fifteen years he spent part of each winter in Australia where he wrote a column for *The Australian*. He also worked for a network of commercial radio stations led by Radio 2UE in Sydney who broadcast an alternative form of commentary for the international games, to the rather more staid government owned ABC. Blowers spent a month or two most years thereabouts in New Zealand where he became a member of the TVNZ commentary team.

Blowers began to write books in 1970. He has written in excess of fifteen titles, mostly about cricket, as well as two autobiographies, *A Thirst for Life* and *Squeezing the Orange*.

His theatrical career began in 2002 when Dudley Russell, a theatre agent and husband of poet Pam Ayres, thought he would be able to do a one-man show. Although cricket inevitably forms a part of these shows, they are really more about the extraordinary life he has led and the fascinating people he has bumped into along the way.

His family name was of course pinched by Ian Fleming for the name of one of his chief villains, Ernst Stavros Blofeld, in the *James Bond* books. He met Fleming who introduced him to Noël Coward at a lunch party in Jamaica. Coward became a friend and Blowers tells some highly amusing stories about him. Clive Dunn, also known as Corporal Jones from the BBC TV series *Dad's Army* was also a friend and another source of some splendid stories.

Blowers also does his share of after dinner speeches, and his distinctive voice has been used for a number of radio and television commercials, and he has also appeared on several TV shows such as the BBC's *Room 101* and ITV's *Celebrity Chase Special*. He also does work for his great friend, David Folb who founded The Lashings World XI, which fields an eleven of international cricketers. They play thirty odd matches a year in England taking famous cricketing names to parts of the country which would never expect to see them. This does a lot to spread the gospel of cricket and is a great boost for the game in the UK.

Lashings go on a short tour each spring to Abu Dhabi where they stay at the Famous Emirates Palace Hotel and play some games on that hotel's beautiful ground.

His cricketing days are fewer now and and he commentates for *Test Match Special* on about twenty-five days Test and International cricket in England each summer and continues to write a few cricket columns a year for the *Daily Express*.

He mainly concentrates these days on his one-man show which has reverberated around Britain's provincial theatres for over a decade. More recently he has also done two-man shows with former *Test Match Special* producer Peter Baxter.

Blowers has also teamed up with John Bly, the furniture expert from *The Antiques Roadshow* who knows more about Chippendale than Chippendale did himself! They performed a two-act show at the 2010 Edinburgh Festival - a chat sitting round the fire with a bottle or two within easy reach, talking about the more ghastly aspects of modern life: political correctness and 'elf 'n safety and the lack of characters in today's world!

Everywhere he has gone, on countless cricket tours around the world, Blowers has lived life to the full regarding each day as an orange and squeezing it dry of the last drop of juice before moving onto the next day.

He is a medical freak having defied a heart by-pass operation which went horribly wrong, a gall bladder that behaved like a deprived monster, picking up the dreaded MRSA along the way. Since then, back and hip operations have followed two-a-penny, but all have been submerged by guffaws of laughter and bottles of Burgundy (both red and white) and life still goes on in capital letters.

Blowers has led a varied, entertaining and extremely full life, has always been, and continues to be outrageous and irresistible fun!

ALSO AVAILABLE

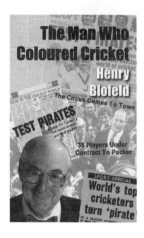

Between 1967-69 Henry Blofeld was fortunate to witness cricket on three continents. He followed the great West Indies side captained by Garry Sobers through its home series against England - to the 1968-9 Australian tour, and finally their early summer '69 tour of England.

Two main themes are explored throughout: The gradual demise of the West Indian side that included the likes of Lance Gibbs, Basil Butcher and Deryck Murray - but which also saw the emergence of future greats such as Clive Lloyd - and the link between a country's topography, style and endemic characteristics with the type of cricket it plays.

These threads are skilfully woven together to highlight great cricketing moments and analyse the humour and style of both the Australians and West Indians with thoughtful insight.

In the late seventies Kerry Packer revolutionised cricket. Today's followers are used to coloured clothing and all the other razzmatazz that is now a part of cricket. But back in 1977 Packer's intervention was divisive and nearly broke the game completely. Players were ostracised by their nations and for a while it looked as if cricket might not survive.

Henry Blofeld observed the goings on from his position as both a commentator and writer. In 1978 he compiled a detailed account of the events that unfolded, aided by his interviews with Packer, as well as the deposed English captain Tony Greig.

The Man Who Coloured Cricket is Blofeld's detailed account of the events of 1977-78. It also shows concern for the human dimensions of the controversy. The varied reaction of the English county players; overseas players; the legal tussles; the complex and surprising character of Packer himself; and the establishment figures with whom he did battle, are strands of the story expertly woven together to make a dramatic and moving story.

Complete with a new afterword in which Henry reappraises his thoughts, The Man Who Coloured Cricket is a truly enthralling read for new and old cricket enthusiasts alike

Cricket on Three Continents
ISBN: 978-1-908724-34-2

The Man Who Coloured Cricket
ISBN: 978-1-908724-35-9

Available from all good retailers. Quote the ISBN if needed.